THE RIVER MERSEY

THE RIVER MERSEY

by

RON FREETHY

Photographs by Robert Smithies

TERENCE DALTON LIMITED
LAVENHAM   .   SUFFOLK
1985

Published by
TERENCE DALTON LIMITED
ISBN 0 86138 035 5

Text photoset in 11/12 pt. Baskerville

Printed in Great Britain at
The Lavenham Press Ltd., Lavenham, Suffolk.

Contents

Acknowledgements vi

Introduction vii

Chapter One   The Mersey and its Source 1

Chapter Two   The Mersey Valley 21

Chapter Three   The Dark River—The Irwell 38

Chapter Four   The Mersey's Canals 59

Chapter Five   The Bollin and the Dean 71

Chapter Six   Irlam to Warrington 90

Chapter Seven   Warrington to the Runcorn Gap 106

Chapter Eight   The River of Salt—The Weaver 116

Chapter Nine   The Cheshire Bank 135

Chapter Ten   The Liverpool Shoreline 151

Bibliography 168

Index 170

Acknowledgements

DURING the production of this book I have been greatly assisted by a band of friends who gathered round to help. John and Nancy Heap, who live near the Manchester Ship Canal, were a constant source of information and ferried me around the area without one word of complaint. Richard Abernethy and Ann Murphy both provided books and encouragement, while Mrs Joyce Lee made known to me the work of her father, James Goodier. The members of Bacup Naturalists pulled my leg and provided old prints of the Irwell, and the team at Halton Chemical Museum were friendly and informative.

Carole Pugh proved invaluable in drawing neat versions of my rough maps and made frequent adjustments to correct my mistakes. Marlene Freethy, my wife, typed the manuscript with her usual patience. Bob Smithies looked at the Mersey with the eye of a photographer, and we are both grateful to Norman Jones, the dark room manager of *The Guardian* and *Manchester Evening News*, who produced a set of lovely prints especially for the book.

I also thank Bob Malster, the publisher's editor, for his tireless efforts, but wish to point out that any errors which remain are purely of my own making.

Thorneyholme Hall,
January 1985.

Introduction

THE IDEA for this book came to me when I announced to a group of friends that I was going bird watching on the Mersey estuary. Their inference was that I should be poisoned and fail to return. None of us knew the river or its tributaries at all well and I determined to see if things were as bad as people thought. I found industry past and present, an abundance of old halls and characters plus a staggering variety of wildlife. Stories in dialect and historical events demanded space and presented the problem of what to leave out.

Some readers may feel that I have attempted too much and have omitted vital areas. I have tried to compensate for this in the bibliography. When Robert Smithies, with whom I have made four films about the Mersey for Granada Television, agreed to take the photographs I was delighted for two reasons. Firstly as the former chief photographer for the *Manchester Guardian* he was sure to produce lovely pictures, but even more importantly his love for the Mersey and its tributaries was as great as mine. Robert's camera followed my own route along footpaths down rivers and canals, through cities, towns and villages and out to sea.

The book has been planned as a journey from source to sea with a number of diversions to follow tributaries back to their source. Such a project would not have been possible without a great deal of help from many people, and these have been listed in the acknowledgements.

PRESTON.

BLACKBURN.

SOUTHPORT.

LEEDS AND LIVERPOOL CANAL.

Rivington Pike.

Ormskirk.

FORMBY

R. ALT.

Aughton.

+ BAR LIGHTSHIP.

Crosby.

WIGAN.

GLAZE BROOK

CHAT

SANKEY BROOK

Croxteth Hall.

Bootle.

Knowsley Hall.

LIVERPOOL

Prescot.

ST HELENS.

Winwick.

Hallasey Seacombe

FERRY

TUNNEL

DITTON BROOK

Sankey.

Warrington.

Bidston Hill

Birkenhead.

Fiddlers Ferry

R. MERSEY.

Warburt

Garston.

Speke Hall.

Port Sunlight.

Oglef. Hale.

Widnes.

MANCHESTER SHIP CANAL

Thelwall.

Bromborough.

Stanlow Priory

Runcorn Halton Weston Point

DUKE of BRIDGEWATERS C

MERE

Eastham.

Frodsham.

GRAND TRUNK CANAL

T KN

Ellesmere Port

Ince.

Helsby.

BUD MERE

HATCHMERE

PICK MERE

R. GOWY

DELAMERE FOREST.

NORTHWICH

Davenham.

Vale Royal Abbey +

Winsford.

SHROPSHIRE UNION CANAL

Tarporley.

Mid

Harthill.

Beeston Castle.

Church Minshull.

R. W

PECKFORTON HILLS.

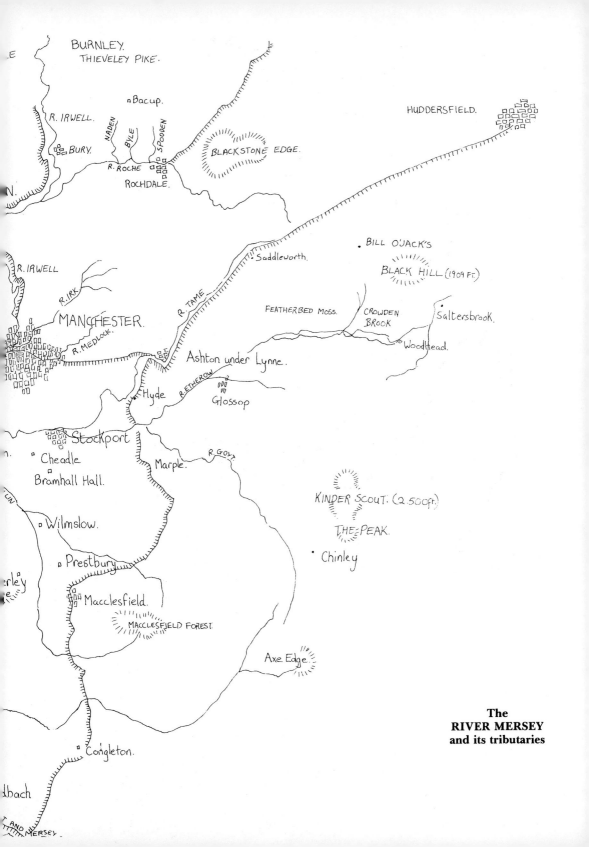

The
RIVER MERSEY
and its tributaries

CHAPTER ONE

The Mersey and its Source

THE RIVER known as the Mersey begins life by forcing itself out of a narrow sandstone gorge near the centre of Stockport. At one time the river formed a natural barrier between the counties of Cheshire and Lancashire; its very name means "boundary river". Life has been tough on the Mersey and there is even some controversy regarding its parentage. Three large tributaries combine to form the Mersey at Stockport. These are the Etherow, the Goyt and the Tame, each having played a significant part in human industry. Each, therefore, has received its share of effluents due both to the industries themselves and to the increased populations which they attracted. By the time these mucky waters have combined heavily polluted slush oozes and oils its way into Stockport.

> Dank and foul, dank and foul
> By the smoky town with its murky cowl
> Foul and dank, foul and dank
> By wharf and river and slimy bank
> Darker and darker the farther I go
> Baser and baser the richer I grow

These lines written by Charles Kingsley perfectly fitted the poor old Mersey which was familiar to the clergyman who wrote *The Water Babies*, and who knew well how to focus a critical eye on the horrors of a fiercely careless industrial age.

Is the situation still as bad? If the Mersey was still a lifeless open sewer this book would be rich in purpose but poor in content. Is all then perfect? Far from it! This work tells the story, sometimes depressing but often heartening, of accelerating efforts by individuals and public bodies to improve the quality of Mersey water. Nowhere have these efforts been more praiseworthy than in the valleys of the three tributaries of Etherow, Goyt and Tame.

The haunting bubbling sound of a courting curlew, its graceful circling flight on winnowing wings, and the song of a soaring lark over the dark mossy boglands typify the birthplace of the Etherow, once said to rise at the junction of the counties of Cheshire, Yorkshire and Lancashire. The

The infant Goyt tumbles over the rocks on its way to
meet the Etherow and the Tame.

1

dale was certainly part of an ancient green road. The Romans built a fort to protect the route taken by Derbyshire lead bound for Chester, and this was still a vital link in the days of pack horse and stage coach, the main cargo then being salt from Cheshire. When the wind howled and snow swept through the valley or when fog confused all but the knowledgeable few this lonely spot must have been hell for the traveller but heaven for the highwayman seeking easy pickings. Little of value can be gained from an argument concerning whether or not the Etherow is the true source of the Mersey; suffice it to say that as long ago as 1226 the "Ederow" as it was then called was given the credit. Controversy, however, was no stranger to the thirteenth century and it is only fair to redress the balance by referring to documents which were written between 1208 and 1229 which indicate that the Goyt is the source. By 1790 historians were becoming more careful and it was noted at that time that the Mersey arose in the Longdendale valley and that its origins were in "different springs about one mile from the Inn called Saltersbrook House within the West Riding of Yorkshire rather more than four miles above the Woodhead."

Salterbrook itself is a feeder stream of the Etherow which bubbles and chuckles its unpolluted way from its source at Red Hole—a boggy moss-studded area—and under the Manchester to Sheffield road to the Etherow, a total distance of around a mile. The district is steeped in folklore, atmosphere and at times fascinating social history. At one time the inn was an essential gathering place for shepherds during early autumn when the "meeting time" sorted out the lost sheep and returned them to their rightful owners. In those times the sheep men really did watch their flocks by night—and by day as well—and they seldom had the time for idle chat. The meet was just the excuse they needed. What yarns must have been spun by these old hands as they sat in the inglenook of the old inn and supped ale in the light of the flickering fire or that from the burning rushlights made from the piths of the plants which grew so abundantly on the hill. Here too would gather the available lasses, their hair blonded by an extract from the roots of bog asphodel, a typical moorland plant glinting like spangled gold from the carpet of spongy sphagnum moss. I wonder if the well-earned refreshment and feminine company softened the shepherd's worry of the highland winter to come which to the lazy, the careless or the downright unlucky could bring disaster and starvation for himself and his dependents. Their life was so simple yet so tough. The building of the Woodhead tunnel to carry the railway link between the expanding cities must have shattered the insular lives of the simple, yet probably contented, shepherds as the avaricious navvies worked, drank and brawled themselves to death, living

The River Etherow flows peacefully in spring as it nears its confluence with the Goyt; a view at Compstall.

out their pitiful lives in shanty towns which have long since crumbled into the hillsides. There is always a price to pay for progress!

Sheep once more have the uplands to themselves, not only around the Salterbrook but also around other Etherow tributaries. There is the once impressive grouse moor around Shelf Brook and the Crowden Brooks which drive through craggy areas of gritstone, the most famous being the Laddow Rocks on which many a famous mountaineer has cut his climbing teeth.

Not only did the great expanding cities need rail links but they also became desperate for water, and the present-day Etherow runs into and out of a series of impressive reservoirs; a look at these reminds the upland walker of the ingenuity of the modern world. Turning the back on these artificial lakes and lifting the eyes to the hills unfolds a view which differs but little from the description rendered by the commissioners who, at the bidding of William the Norman, compiled the Domesday book. In 1086 they pointed out that

> The whole of Longendale is waste. The wood there is not pasturable. Fit only for hunting. The whole VIII miles in length and IV in breadth, value XL shillings.

Most, if not all, of the beasts of the hunt have gone, but man having accomplished this, nature was left in peace until the industrial revolution and the manufacture of textiles which demanded two things, fast-moving water and a damp climate. The Etherow, in company with the other northern valleys, had both these in good measure and manufacturing towns rapidly sprang up along its banks. The reservoirs of Woodhead, Torside, Rhodeswood, Valehouse and the appropriately named Bottoms through which the Etherow flowed ensured even in dry summers a regular water supply to the towns in the valleys below. Some idea of how impressive this scheme must have been can be gauged from the fact that in 1877 they constituted the largest area of artificial water in the world. The three-and-half-million-pound bill was thought to be worth it as some twenty-four million gallons of water was diverted to the thirsty city of Manchester.

Most of the once-prosperous mills have now had their day and, indeed, it would seem that the Etherow was less industrialised than either the Goyt or the Tame. There were some important, and in the context of their day, some mightily impressive mills, and it is around one of these that the successful Etherow Country Park has been based. Credit for this brave venture must go to the Bredbury and Romiley Urban District Council (now swallowed by the Stockport Metropolitan Borough Council) who developed the site around Compstall Mill, which began weaving cotton in 1826 and closed as recently as 1966. The reservoir which is so much a feature of the park was built by the Andrews family to power a number of cotton mills, and areas once humming with cog and flywheel now echo to the metallic chatterings of coot and the slap of rope on hull as apprentice sailors are put through their paces. The entrance to the park is one mile (1½ km) north-east of Marple on the B6104 road, and there are ample car parking, toilet and refreshment facilities and a friendly and efficient wardening service.

The park has been produced from two separate elements. Firstly the cotton mill with its associated lodges, reservoirs and weirs has proved an ideal habitat for native waterfowl such as mallard, tufted duck and pochard and also introduced species such as the delightfully attractive mandarin ducks and the princely Canada geese. Kingfishers often sparkle in the sunshine while coot and moorhen are common. In the area of the river just prior to the weir the retained water has the effect of increasing the depth and slowing the flow, thus producing another ideal area for waterfowl. By 1971 the park was taking shape and since this time industrial effluent has decreased and management efficiency of such areas improved to such an extent that this area of the Etherow must be more attractive to wildfowl than it has ever been.

The second element of the country park, which covers 162 acres (65½ hectares), is known as the Keg woodlands. Keg House was initially a hunting lodge surrounded by extensive areas of woodland used by those who wished to shoot game, but happily the only shooting now faced by the collection of game birds (kept in aviaries) is that of visitors' cameras. The woodlands contain Scots pine, Wych elm, hazel, ash, oak and sycamore, and the acrobatic grey squirrel occasionally entertains the visitors with its attractive antics. One particularly sensible provision is that of a private nature reserve on the eastern bank of the river which is administered by the Cheshire Naturalists' Trust; since it is not open to the public it gives the birds the peace and quiet they need to breed and protects the plants from the innocent but still heavy feet of the visitors. The ornithologist will find dippers present all the year round; swallows, swifts and martins are common summer visitors, while in winter the wildfowl counts are more impressive each year. Visitors arriving by car need to remember to carry some ten pence pieces, as exit from the park is via a coin-operated barrier.

The country park is, so to speak, the Etherow's last glorious stand, for just beyond this point it flows into Brabyns Park, where it is joined by the Goyt; and its name disappears, leaving the Goyt to flow into Marple Dale. Brabyns Park is famous for its dog cemetery and a rather attractive iron bridge which crosses the Goyt near a house of the same name. Just beyond this the two rivers join at the appropriately named Watersmeeting.

The Goyt

A high wind howled across the moors and my car headlights stabbed through the early morning sleet; an earlier more persistent fall of snow contrasted sharply with the outcrops of dark satanic gritstone. A light flashed from a gap in a curtained window of the *Cat and Fiddle Inn* and the sounds of life emerging from slumber after a cool early spring night made the scene decidedly less dismal. A dog barked and sheep called to each other across the soft bogs and picked their way skilfully across the more solid ground. As I followed them towards the soggy source of the Goyt the smell of heather crushed beneath my boots killed for a moment the choking fumes of hydrogen sulphide from the rotting vegetation and brought back memories of summer when bilberry gives up its rich bounty

A notice reminds visitors to the Peak District National Park that it is lambing time in the Goyt Valley and that the animals should be left undisturbed.

and young grouse practise their first tentative flights in the late evening sun. The dominant plant of the damper areas is without doubt the sphagnum moss, bleached white when dried in the summer sun but green and as absorbent as a sponge after rain. This latter quality doubtless led to its use as a wound dressing in ancient times and even during the First World War. Its efficiency in this respect was considerably increased by the fact that it is also a powerful astringent. Add to this the fact that bacteria are killed by the acidic breakdown products in bugs and we must conclude that sphagnum is much more sterile than the average bandage which has been carried around in an often grubby backpack.

As the Goyt's waters gather and widen, the need for bridging them to carry important trade routes into Derbyshire must have been obvious from the earliest days of organised human commerce. Close to the *Cat and Fiddle* is the gritstone Derbyshire Bridge standing on the old boundary with Cheshire; its charm comes not because it is pretty but because of the easy intimacy with which it fits into the local scenery. In the days of salt smuggling—until the eighteenth century there was a high tax on this essential commodity—the Goyt's packhorse bridge was another vital link in the trade routes. Its importance is not readily appreciated today because much of the area it served is now swamped beneath the Errwood reservoir, built in the 1960s, and beyond it is the larger Fernilee reservoir. The loss to pure historians has been somewhat compensated for by the gain to natural historians as wildfowl, not typically a feature of the upper Goyt, are taking advantage of this new stretch of water, despite the presence of a sailing club. At one time there was a possibility that Goyt's bridge itself would be submerged, but a compromise was reached and it was moved stone by gritstone to its present position further down the valley.

Derbyshire has long been a focal point for weekend trippers, and the novelty of the bridge proved so irresistible that each of the three narrow lanes which led to the bridge became snarled with angry traffic. A solution was urgently needed, and a controversial one was eventually found which involved the provision of car parking on the fringes and the declaration of a motor-free zone in the vicinity of the bridge at peak times and a one-way system at others. Considering that over seventeen million people live within a fifty-mile radius of the peak and that the district attracts more than ten million visitors each year, it is clear that such a move was not a case of "red tape gone mad"; a survey revealed that ninety per cent of visitors agreed with the plan. To help the elderly and infirm, the provision of a limited mini-bus service from the car parks into the heart of the dale provided the final link in a sensible compromise. Another car park is close by Jenkin Chapel, also known as St. John's church, which was built in 1733 and which dominates a stretch of ancient road known as The Street which was the old salt road from Cheshire into Derbyshire. A mini-bus service operates from here into the Goyt valley.

The area beyond the bridge is Goytsclough Quarry, which deserves an honorary mention in the annals of migratory men. The once rich Thomas Pickford made a series of disastrous decisions during the period of the Civil War in the middle of the seventeenth century, but recovered by quarrying road stone. It is said that at one time the world's largest waterwheel, powered by the sprightly waters of the Goyt, operated machinery that broke stone into manageable lumps, and soon the streets of the expanding town of Macclesfield were paved with Pickford stones. Londoners soon wished to have their streets similarly paved with stone to lift the garments of the wealthy above the mud, the gold having run out long before the arrival of Dick Whittington! Pickford by the 1680s was back in the big time, but carting stone was a long hard trip. Even then time meant money, and bringing back an empty cart meant loss of revenue. Pickford advertised for cargo for the return journey, and the removal firm so founded has been thriving ever since.

The once busy scene is now somewhat muted, especially during winter, a summer weekday or early in the morning. The Derbyshire Bridge car park is signed to the left off the A537 just beyond *The Cat and Fiddle*. A pleasant stroll will bring you to what is left of the once substantial Errwood Hall; the old rhododendrons and azaleas still bloom in splendid isolation. You can still just make out the ruins of a couple of impressive wings flanking a central tower, and the once fountained gardens are now a mixture of exotic and indigenous wildwoods. Rabbits feed with flicking ears searching for the sound of the cunning weasels which lurk in the old lichen-encrusted walls hanging with ferns such as polypody, spleenwort and wall rue. Errwood Hall clough still attracts birds, including long tailed tits and the woodcock with their huge staring eyes. As the long bill probes into the soft areas of damp woodland the woodcock would not be well served by accurate vision straight in front of it; it does need to be able to see any predator approaching from the side or rear, and its eyes are therefore set at the side of the head. The large size of the eyes allows a good intake of light, enabling the woodcock to see in areas of low light intensity—very useful for a bird living in the shade of a summer forest.

In the days before the building of the reservoirs to quench the thirst of the expanding Stockport the marshlands were of greater extent and breeding herons were a feature of the woodlands, although the exact population has not been recorded. The heron's loss is the gull's and wildfowl's gain, and while the reservoir is not as ornithologically rich as many, it still serves as a resting place for wildfowl on migration and as a safe roost for the expanding population of gulls waxing fat, here as elsewhere, on the rich pickings of the refuse dumps of our throw-away society.

On the journey to its union first with the Etherow and then with the Tame before becoming the Mersey, the Goyt picks up a number of important tributaries. From the west around Whaley Bridge the Todd Brook tumbles down some precipitous slopes from its source near the 1830 foot (558 metre) summit of Shining Tor, only a couple of miles from where the Goyt itself oozes through the sphagnum. Another tributary rises in the Peak Forest around Sparrow pit and feeds through a set of reservoirs and thence to Chapel-en-le-Frith and Chinley. The name Chapel-en-le-Frith is Norman in origin and means the Chapel in the Forest clearing, the first such structure being built in 1225 and dedicated to Thomas Becket. The present settlement has a lovely cobbled market square dominated by a seventeenth century cross and stocks. The highest point of Kinder Scout (2058 feet— 627 metres) spawns the Kin, and this is joined by the Sett close to Hayfield.

This was once one of the most industrialised of the tributaries, dammed for water and damned by effluents from textile mills and scouring plants and by raw domestic sewage. The breakdown of this excrement is effected by bacteria which require oxygen extracted from the water, leaving it deficient in this vital commodity. The invertebrate organisms in the water and the fish which depend upon them die and decay, a process demanding even more oxygen. Light cannot penetrate what is now an open sewer and the death of the plant life which depends upon it adds to the misery of the watercourse. Things have improved

The River Tame, on the right, is crossed at Ashton-under-Lyne by the Peak Forest Canal aqueduct. The Ashton Canal can be seen in the left foreground.

dramatically in recent years, due partly to more efficient sewage treatment works, a decline in industry and also happily due to an increased effort to clean up our polluted rivers. The Sett Valley Trail passes through the sites of many of these old industries, including a printworks which once used wood blocks to print textiles, once a huge calico mill. Also close by is Birch Hall, once a house of some importance but now a hotel named the *Waltzing Weasel*. Another ex-printworks at Birch Vale is a favourite spot of anglers, who enjoy good sport in the mill lodges.

To the east above Taxal and Whaley Bridge stands the soggy mass of Combs Moss, with the inevitable dark outcroppings of gritstone. On the many days of low cloud and swirling mists it takes little imagination to conjure up images of the Hound of the Baskervilles and other bloodcurdling Victorian melodramas. Despite the decelerating effect of

The Marple aqueduct which takes the Peak Forest Canal over the River Goyt. In the background a train crosses the railway viaduct.

the Combs reservoir, the stream is impressive as it reaches the Goyt, helping the Todd and the Kin, along with other smaller watercourses, to drain this area of Macclesfield Forest. The moor and valley was once held in the fierce feudal grip of the Downes family, who may be regarded as the northern equivalent of the Doones. They were both judge and jury with the legal right to hang, draw and quarter those whom they found guilty. There is a grisly reminder that this right was sometimes exercised at a spot called Gallows Yard near Overton.

Once the waters of Goyt have absorbed those of the Etherow at Brabyns Park it continues towards Marple and passes under the substantial arches of the aqueduct carrying the Peak Forest Canal. The Marple aqueduct is less than a mile from the town centre, is around 308 feet (94 metres) long and is supported on three massive arches. Its water trough is lined not with brick but with iron. When it was opened in 1800 the designers, Outram and Brown, were at the mercy of their many critics but time has supported their theory and it is hard to decide which is the greater engineering achievement, the aqueduct itself or the staircase of sixteen locks which reduces the canal level by a staggering 200 feet. Although within easy reach of the centre of Manchester, Marple has not lost the atmosphere of a small self-sufficient market town. Part of the Wildwood remains, and the houses are set neatly around the ravine through which the Goyt spurts on its way to the old watermeadows and fertile fields beyond. This alluvial farmland has long served as a market garden for Manchester and Stockport.

Just off the A627 east of Stockport is Chadkirk Country Park, which is remarkable in the sense that it is centred on a working farm of some 59 acres (24 hectares). The complex of farm and chapel was purchased by the go-ahead Bredbury and Romiley Urban District Council, but was taken over by the Metropolitan Borough of Stockport, which opened it in 1979 as a country park. Visitors should not enter the farm buildings, but there is no real need to interfere since the trail leaflet and well sited notice boards provide all relevant information. Part of the thrill of the walk is to watch the workings of a real farm run at a profit rather than a museum lacking the essential ingredient—incentive! The old chapel has been converted to function as a visitors' centre and there are several well-sited picnic tables. Close to the farm trail car park a stile leads to Kirkwood, which has an excellent picnic area overlooking a pleasant weir.

Another interesting site close to the Goyt is that of the so-called Roman Lakes. These are, in fact, of a much later vintage and provided a reservoir for Oldknow's Mill, which was near Bottom's Bridge. The lakes are now put to a much more pleasurable use as anglers and those who enjoy a peaceful row will testify.

Gradually the local councils of Tameside, Stockport and Manchester are pooling resources and expertise to produce linked footpaths which it is hoped will eventually encourage adventurous walkers to walk from Goyt to Etherow and on into Tameside. Few river valleys can have been more devastated by industry than the Tame and few can, in recent years, boast of more dedicated workers bent on restoring purity and beauty to a much abused watercourse.

The Tame

The word Tame is of Celtic origin and has its root in Tamh, which means broad or spreading, although some workers have suggested that it means dark river. This origin also accounts for the name of other rivers including the Teme, the Tamar and Old Father Thames himself. The Tame, rising to the east of Manchester and north-east of the charming old village of Denshaw in Saddleworth, can truly be regarded as a curate's egg of a river. Many sections along its twenty-mile journey to the Mersey are clear and twinkling but other stretches, sadly still in a majority, are very bad indeed. Would the Tame still be so polluted if it flowed through Westminster? I doubt it!

> I was bred on the cold grey hills,
> In the days when life was stern
> When work had left the old handlooms
> And wages were hard to earn.
>
> And lean days gripped my father's hearth
> With nothing to spend on books
> And the little I know was learned
> From the folks in the ingle nooks.

These words were written by Ammon Wrigley, who was born at Saddleworth in 1862 and like the rest of the artisan poets was well used to hard graft. He knew and revelled in spots of rare beauty, and worried about the increasing ill-treatment and pollution of others.

From Saddleworth the Tame works its way through Mossley, Stalybridge, Dukinfield, Ashton-under-Lyne and Hyde and flows thence to Stockport, where it joins the Goyt under a tangle of functional, unimaginative concrete known as the Mersey Way. The valley is dominated by millstone grit, along with blocks of sandstone, but between them are mudstones and shales, the whole sandwich formed by the infilling of a once extensive marine basin. All this happened 280 million years ago, the whole geological complex being around 700 metres thick! Many streams, each in its own valley, feed the Tame, the most important being the Diggle, Chew and Carr Brooks, each of which now carries its share of industrial and faecal effluent. The watershed of the Tame is close to that of the Medlock, an important tributary of the Irwell (see Chapter Three).

Saddleworth is a fascinating spot, although strictly speaking there is no such place, the name being an umbrella for a series of historic villages, surprisingly attractive in view of their industrial origins. Dobcross, Diggle and Delph is not a firm of solicitors but three of these villages, the former being used as the set for the film "Yanks" since it has changed so little since Hitler's War. Its winding street climbs steeply to the village square and has a charm all of its own. Uppermill is the focal point of the area and it is here that the secondary school is sited. The village boasts a splendid little museum illustrating the history and natural history of the valley. Many authoritative leaflets have been produced by the Saddleworth Historical Society, including village trail guides to Uppermill itself,

THE RIVER TAME

Denshaw, Delph, Heights and Grange as well as to the Huddersfield Narrow Canal which cuts through the area. Great strides have been made to improve the valley, which was virtually destroyed by unbridled industrial exploitation with no thought for anything other than quick profits for a very privileged few, who were not usually "bred on the cold grey hills".

The year 1969 saw the inauguration of the "Tame Valley Improvement Scheme" which involved the Civic Trust for the North West, Greater Manchester County, Stockport, Tameside and Oldham Councils and last but by no means least the North West Water Authority and the British Waterways Board. The leaflet *The Tame Valley* clearly identified the problem, which will take years and cost many millions of pounds to solve. Progress has, however, already been made and the leaflet points out that

> The landscape of the valley will only survive with care and attention. Of increasing concern to the Tame Valley Joint Committee is the management and maintenance of the open spaces in the valley. The Committee now controls and develops these aspects directly through the Warden service which is equipped to carry out minor repairs in the valley, backed up by a competent maintenance service, as well as policing, protecting and promoting the use of the valley with the help of voluntary wardens.

Conservation

Just as its landscape is receiving particular attention, so the valley's rich architectural heritage is benefiting from a positive approach to conservation and restoration. This can be seen in villages like Delph or Dobcross, the industrial archaeology of canals (in particular the recently improved Portland Basin) and the attention given to individual buildings of note such as Newton Hall at Dukinfield and the Millgate Centre at Delph.

Elsewhere, any development in or visible from the valley calls for a particularly high standard of design to complement the purpose of the Tame Valley Improvement Scheme.

School Involvement

The impetus of the Tame Valley Improvement Scheme has encouraged voluntary workers, under the guidance of the Tame Valley Warden, to clean out the river and canals, and generally tidy up the areas in the valley. A number of simple but helpful tasks have been performed by working parties of schoolchildren in the valley. Under the supervision of the Tame Valley Wardens, children participate in such work as cleaning through woodlands and tree planting in the appropriate season.

The valley is an ideal classroom for the local schools and it is already being used as a centre for practical study. At Hartshead Power Station a particularly enlightened approach to nature conservation and education by the Central Electricity Generating Board has led to the establishment of a well-equipped field study centre for use by the children. This site, rich in flora and fauna, has a full time warden. The Civic Trust for the North West and the Tame Valley Wardens are available to lecture schools and local societies, and an ever increasing wealth of visual information is also available for use in conjunction with these activities.

Recreation in the Tame Valley

The improvements carried out over the last few years have made large areas in the Tame Valley attractive and accessible. A number of these areas in the valley lend themselves particularly well to the development of specific recreational pursuits.

The canals throughout the valley provide excellent opportunities for recreation. The Lower Peak Forest Canal and the Ashton Canal, now cleaned and renovated, allow the passage of pleasure craft on a system of over 100 miles of navigable waterways known as the Cheshire Ring.

The Huddersfield Narrow Canal is not navigable but has been made safe and attractive; the locks have been cascaded and cleaned and parts of the towpath have been restored. The ambitious long term proposal of the Huddersfield Narrow Canal Society is to try and re-open the canal for navigation.

The clean water in the canals and the scattering of well stocked mill lodges and reservoirs along the valley gives ample opportunity for fishing, and they are extensively used by local angling clubs.

The canals in the valley meet at Portland Basin. The basin still retains much of its original canal architecture, and the possibility of establishing this area as an attractive centre for land and water-based recreation is being actively pursued.

The upper reaches of the river in Saddleworth are clean and sparkling and pleasant walks along the banks above Uppermill show what the lower valley will be like when the river is clean. The reservoirs in the Pennine foothills could be more extensively used to cater for specific recreational requirements, similar to the yachting club based at Dovestones.

The valley is criss-crossed by footpaths which enable the natural beauty of the scenery to be appreciated. Many are well-trod and a programme for maintenance of them is being prepared. Existing footpaths will be augmented by new ones to create a continuous waterside walk accessible from surrounding built-up areas. Information on valley walks is to be made available through pamphlets and information signs.

Horse-riding and cycling are popular in the valley, and where possible safe bridlepaths are being created on disused railway lines to take the strain off the existing footpath network and allow people to make use of the large open spaces in the valley.

The rural nature of the valley lends itself to these informal pursuits. The valley is there to be used and enjoyed whether it is for a Sunday evening stroll or for kids just fooling about. In many places it is big enough and green enough to seem miles away from the surrounding built-up areas. However, there are also strong pressures to accommodate more organised, recreational uses and these need to be considered against the demands made by other non-recreational activities and the need to safeguard the attractive environment of the valley.

A place must be left for wildlife, and if this is to be secure in the future pollution must be brought to heel. The sheer magnitude of the problem was highlighted in a document *The Tame Valley Water Pollution* financed by the Civic Trust for the North West. This points out that in 1971 the river had to cope with the excrement produced by a human population of around 375,000. Until it reaches Chew Brook the Tame is so clear that it is given the status of a class I river and has a few areas of quite good trout fishing. On its often tortured journey from Chew to Stockport the so-called B.O.D. level reaches a lethal level at several points close to sewage outfalls, but improves a little in the zones in between. The Biological Oxygen Demand rises when the sewage discharged into it is broken down by bacteria which require oxygen to do this and thus little is left over for aquatic wildlife. By the time the Tame has reached Stalybridge it is in a very poor state and in many areas it is nothing short of an open sewer. At Dukinfield the river is forty per cent effluent, while in Stockport it feeds the poor old Mersey with twenty-five per cent pure water plus a staggering seventy-five per cent effluent. The construction of a chain of new sewage treatment works will eventually reduce the B.O.D., as will the removal of the number of storm overflow channels which in heavy rain can discharge sewage into the river without any treatment at all.

With such problems to face it is a wonder that any wildlife exists at all, yet there is still such a rich variety along parts of the river that one is left with nothing but amazement at the sheer resilience of nature. As the problems are slowly overcome it is also surprising to find how quickly plants and then animals which depend either directly or indirectly upon them return. Ironically the effects of "moderate" sewage pollution in the river itself may have the effect of improving the vegetation on the banks of the river. The unpleasant looking faeces deposited along the banks in times of spate acts as a most efficient fertiliser and an assortment of docks, hogweed, false oat grass, himalayan balsam, butterbur, mugwort and nettle all thrive.

It is amusing to think that in the "good old days" nettles were cultivated as a vegetable, and when cotton was a fabric of the future nettle fibre was woven into fabric. The plant demands high levels of nitrogen in the soil and this is why it grows well in our modern, sewage-polluted, world. The seeds of these and other plants, particularly the plantains, provide food for birds in the short days of autumn and early winter, while in summer the rank herbage offers an ideal nesting habitat. Reed buntings, linnets, greenfinches and an increasing number of goldfinches find good habitat here, while pied wagtails push their way through the murky looking shallows and are apparently able to scratch a living. In the heavily polluted areas few organisms can survive due to the high B.O.D., but the larva of the hoverfly has solved the problem. Instead of absorbing its oxygen directly from the water, the animal has evolved a long tube which it pushes out of the water surface so that oxygen is sucked in directly from the atmosphere. This long tube has earned the hover fly larva the alternative name of rat-tailed maggot. The brown rat has made the polluted reaches of the Tame, and the Mersey itself, its home, and even raw sewage is consumed by this ever-hungry, fast-breeding, rodent which only reached Britain in the middle eighteenth century. In rivers devastated by pollution the rat is just one more cross to bear; it can spread disease, and the tunnels it makes in the river banks can cause drainage problems. We must, however, not blame the rat for simply exploiting the conditions which we have created.

The writer must also take care not to paint all of the river with the same polluted brush. Some areas are clear and abound with wildlife, especially in the stretches above Greenfield. In the swift stretches hereabouts the river is coloured by liverworts such as *Scapania* and the splendid greenery of *Fontinalis*, the water moss. Dippers and grey wagtails search, each in its own unique way, for aquatic creatures, the former looking like a dumpy wren with a white bib, bobbing up and down on stones like an accomplished ballet dancer. There are two

The River Tame and Park Road Mill at Dukinfield. The river here contains as much as forty per cent effluent.

possible explanations for this bobbing action. Some workers suggest that the movement affords camouflage against the moving water while others feel that it helps the dipper focus on its food in the water before plunging into the current. Birds do not have binocular vision because of the wide positioning of their eyes, and head movements do improve the perception of distance. While the dipper is able to submerge its whole body, the grey wagtail concentrates on the shallows and hops from stone to stone, its long tail helping its incredible sense of balance. To the colour of the birds is added the golden flash from monkey flower and the sky blue of water forget-me-not, while the air is often perfumed by the delicate aroma of the purple-flowered water mint. This is rather stronger than garden mint, but a sprig added to a pan of boiling potatoes does improve the flavour.

As one follows the Tame from source to Mersey industry is often intrusive, but none of the towns through which it passes is particularly large and most have kept some of their historic halls and churches.

> The river that runs by the old hall's walls,
> Murmured to them as it murmurs now.
> The golden glow of sunset falls,
> As it did for them, on glade, river and bough.
> The hall where they feasted, the church where they prayed,
> Their cradles and chambers, and gravestones stay,
> While lord and vassel, youth and maid
> Knight and lady, have passed away.

The hall referred to here in Thomas Middleton's *Annals of Hyde and District* has almost, but fortunately not quite, gone the same way. The site of the old Arden (or Harden) Hall was built upon as long ago as 1350 by Peter de Arderne, who came into possession of the land by intermarriage with the Bredbury family. Looking at the O.S. map, Castle Hill close to the site of Arden Hall indicates that an ancient castle or perhaps a hill

The Huddersfield Canal emerging at Mossley, which in the nineteenth century grew into a booming cotton town. Now much of its industry has gone.

fort stood overlooking the Tame. The watch tower is all that now remains of the once impressive but now ruined hall. It is known locally as Cromwell's Castle, as Oliver is supposed to have stayed there during the Civil War. It can be viewed from the Reddish Vale Trail which begins in a tiny wood signed off Stockport Road, Denton. The walk begins close to a sewage works and ends some three and a half miles (5.6 km) later close to the Arden Arms. The trail itself is rich in wildlife, but for lovers of old halls there can be few to beat it. Hyde Hall farm is signed at the start of the trail. Until the early years of the nineteenth century the hall belonged to the Hydes of Denton, who could claim among their forebears such dignitaries as Edward Hyde, Chancellor to Charles II, who bestowed upon him the title of Earl of Clarendon. One of his daughters, Anne Hyde, was the mother of two English Queens. Anne was the first wife of the ill-fated James II, and her daughter Mary ruled with her husband William and was succeeded by her sister Anne. The timber-framed Hyde Hall deserves to be a listed building in its own right, even if the rumour that Anne stayed here while she was Queen is not true, although she may well have visited it as a child. Although the Hydes of Hyde have now long gone the building, used as a farmhouse, is still full of character. Many would prefer these old houses to be lived in and earn their keep rather than serve as rate-supported nine-to-five museums.

Reddish Vale also cradled two other ancient halls. The place itself got its name from Robert de Reddish, who settled here in 1181, his descendants remaining at Reddish Hall until 1613. Woodhall which overlooked the Tame was part of the family estate. Industry came to the rural scene before 1800, principally in the form of a calico printing works which used power from the Tame and compensation water from specially constructed millponds locally called "flashes". According to the excellent booklet produced by the Tame Valley Warden Service "The initial method of printing was by hand using wooden blocks, until machine printing was introduced .... using copper rollers". The Calico Printers Association bought the mill in 1899, by which time there were thirteen printing machines in the mill and 330 people were employed.

The Tame Valley Warden Service is also responsible for a number of other trail booklets full of information for the natural and conventional historian. The Roaches Trail winds for an impressive one and a half miles (2.4 km) during which it traces the development of Mossley from a modest settlement of around 1,200 in 1821 to a booming cotton town of the 1880's supporting 15,000 people. The trail itself is sandwiched between the old London and North Western Railway track from Manchester to London and the present Manchester to Leeds line. Much industry has gone and trout have returned to the Tame, while the Sugar

Well continues to provide good spring water reputed to have medicinal properties. The Royal George Mills are set into a belt of trees and the hilltops are crowned by the Pots and Pans War Memorial, so called because the rocks are shaped like pots and pans, to the north-east and Wharmton Hill television mast due north. Woodcock flit in and out of the trees and grey wagtails find flies to eat, especially in the area where flies are attracted to the effluent.

Of all the townships along the valley of the Tame, Stalybridge is perhaps the best example of the way industry affected the once oak-wooded valley. An earth fort at Buckton Hill was built by the Celts some time after 500 BC, and it seems likely that a Roman road ran from Melandra (Wooley Bridge) to Cattleshaw, local historians thinking that this way is more logical than the shorter eastern route since at Stalybridge there was a ford. The name of the town almost certainly derives from the Stayley or Stavelegh family, whose home was at Staley Hall, which still stands. The present building was planned in the form of an E which indicates its tudor origins, but it was built on the site of an earlier structure dating back to 1343. John Wesley is said to have preached at Staley Hall in the momentous year of 1745 when the Jacobites were marching south.

The North's nineteenth century cotton boom owes much to a lad from Stalybridge. In the churchyard is buried Neddy Hall, who in 1776 built the first cotton mill in the valleys sited in Word Street, near where the 'bus station is now. The mill is gone, but Neddy Hall must take credit for another innovation, the first steam-powered mill in the county. The six horse power engine which James Watt designed needed a tall chimney to disperse the billowing smoke. Thus the first of thousands of chimneys, known then as Sootpokes, rose above the lines of the valleys. The engines were known for many years as "Old Neds" and the locals then as now were not slow to put their thoughts into verse, as an old ballad illustrates.

> They said "owd Ned turned every wheel
> An every wheel a strap"
> By gum I thinks to mysel
> 'owd Ned's a rare strong chap.

Stalybridge has lost much of its cotton industry and now concentrates on light engineering, its river is cleaner and its civic amenities are many including the 60-acre Stamford Park and Cheetham Park bird sanctuary. The River Tame, however, is still heavily polluted as it makes its way to the ancient town of Stockport and its union with Etherow and Goyt to form the Mersey. We should not forget that much of the Victorians' brass, as well as the muck, had its origins on the banks of the main tributary of the Mersey, the River Tame.

CHAPTER TWO

The Mersey Valley

ONCE THE Mersey has been formed from its three tributaries its course is impossible to follow through the town centre of Stockport due to a remarkable piece of early twentieth century engineering which culverted the river under the complex shopping area called the Mersey Way.

When the river has emerged once more into daylight it is squeezed through a high sandstone gorge, a natural feature which even the hand of man has not completely tamed. This early stretch is overlooked by a series of caves which served as shelters during the 1939-45 war when Stockport's closeness to the industries of Manchester brought the horror of systematic bombing.

Stockport was an important point on the Roman road between Manchester and Buxton, and in view of this it is rather surprising that it does not appear in the Domesday Book. Despite this omission the Normans must have recognised its strategic importance because they built a castle on the site of a Roman fort (dated around AD 50) which Gilbert de Constantine defended against Henry II. For many years the building was the refuge of the Earls of Chester, and the part it played in the Civil War led to its demolition. Prince Rupert with his Cavalier forces routed the Parliamentarians at Stockport in 1644, but his victory was evidently short lived and the Roundheads had regained control of the town by the following year. After the war the castle, whose site lies beneath the market place, was dismantled and the town enjoyed a period of peace, but in 1745 Stockport was on Bonnie Prince Charlie's line of march and all the bridges crossing the Mersey were blown up.

Few old buildings have survived in a town which played such a large role in the "muck and brass" days of the industrial revolution, but those which have survived are indeed impressive. One of these, a half timbered building, stands on the old Roman road, now called Great Underbank Street, and serves as a bank. The name of the building is easy enough to remember, it is how to spell it which presents the problem. Arderne, Arden, or Harden House dates to the late fifteenth century and for over 300 years was the town house of the Arderne family. They were believed to be related to William Shakespeare through his mother, Mary Arden. Some alterations have been made to the Tudor building, especially in the eighteenth century when a splendid oak staircase and a curved chimney

piece were added. Fortunately the hall is now in good hands, but in any event it is now a listed building and its future is secure—or ought to be. This is just as well, as the old town needs to keep all its old buildings.

The loss of some of its historic buildings is the price Stockport has had to pay for being the largest town in Cheshire and for its growing rich not only on cotton but also on chemicals, felt hats and its engineering expertise. Competition during the aggressive commercial days of Victorian Britain was fierce, and it was no wonder that the town's M.P., Richard Cobden, did so much to push the Free Trade Acts through Parliament. His town's gratitude is expressed as an impressive bronze statue in St. Peter's Square.

Students of Old Stockport must be prepared to visit the parish church of St. Mary the Virgin and Vernon park museum. The church is basically early nineteenth century, most of its structure dating from 1810 to 1816. A surprisingly successful attempt was made, however, to retain as many ancient artefacts as possible and in the chancel are many fourteenth century fragments. The parish records are fascinating, especially one unique piece of seventeenth century vandalism. There is a verse scratched on the wall by John Bradshaw, who was born at Marple Hall and baptised at Stockport on 18th December, 1602. The third son of Henry Bradshaw, he received his education at Middleton, Bunbury and at Macclesfield Chantry Grammar School (see chapter five). The rough but prophetic verse he scratched on the wall of Macclesfield church said

My brother Henry must heir the land
My brother Frank must be at his command;
While I, poor Jack will do that
That all the world must wonder at.

After a period as a clerk to a Congleton lawyer John Bradshaw sought, and gained, his fortune in London, being called to the Bar at Gray's Inn in 1627. He returned to Congleton and was mayor of the town in 1637.

He never made any secret of his dislike of the monarchy and his wish for the institution of a republic, but it is unlikely that the boy who scratched his name on the wall of his school church realised the form that his boyish boast would take, for John Bradshaw was the first and only commoner in British history to sentence his reigning Monarch to death and to see the sentence carried out. Bradshaw's name is the first on King Charles' death warrant, and on the freezing morning of 30th January, 1649, the head of Charles Stuart was hacked from his shoulders. Against the record of John Bradshaw's birth in the Stockport church register an unknown hand has scrawled the word "traitor".

The start of the Mersey at Stockport, whose parish church of St Mary the Virgin looks down on the infant river.

Vernon park museum is only about half a mile from the market, sited on the crest of a hill from which the Mersey valley and all the hills among which its tributaries rise can be seen. Few museums cater so well for the geologist and the naturalist, and the bird collection is particularly fine. The most impressive feature of all, however, is a window made up of around 250 pieces of fluorspar which came from the Blue John mine at Castleton in the Derbyshire hills. This was the work of John Tym, who was a native of Castleton and as curator of Vernon park museum was able to forge a lasting link between his places of birth and employment. Anyone who wishes to know about the geology of the Mersey will find this museum the ideal place to begin; students of industrial archeology will find fascination in the mills and some of the great chimneys which remain. These are either illustrated in the museum itself or can be seen from the vantage point on which it stands. Students of Stockport should not—indeed cannot—miss the austere but magnificent railway viaduct which looks down on the town. Its twenty-two arches carry the line a distance of 1,800 feet at a height of 108 feet above town and Mersey, a phenomenal feat of engineering which must have been the wonder of its age.

Stockport is often described as an ugly conurbation, a grossly

unfair description. I would prefer to describe it as a place of contrasts. The railway viaduct is a perfect example of the Victorians' ability to relate structure to function, just as the Tudors' hallmark was gracious living. Bramhall Hall, acquired by Stockport council and open from Tuesday to Sunday each week except in December, has been described as the most impressive black and white manor house in England. No one approaching along the winding rhododendron-lined drive to the atmospheric building built in the fifteenth century by the Bramhale family could possibly doubt its claim. From the Bramhales the house passed by marriage to the Davenports. The finest possession still in the house is a magnificent seventeenth century tapestry showing the Fall of Man which represents thirty-six years of patient, eye-straining work by Dame Dorothy Davenport. This lady and her husband Sir William must have loved their home, because they carried out some sensitive rebuilding around 1600. In 1819 more alterations and rebuilding were carried out without disrupting the Tudor fabric.

The great hall, constructed of huge arched timbers, may be even older than the fifteenth century and be part of an earlier Bramhall Hall. Another gem is the oak spiral staircase leading to a magnificent Elizabethan drawing room with a fireplace of such huge dimensions that

A contrast in lifestyles: on the opposite page the fine Tudor Bramhall Hall, one of the most impressive timber-framed buildings in the country, and on the right caves in the sandstone of the Mersey Gorge.

with a blazing log fire filling the grate no-one could possibly have been cold even in the hardest frosts. The room also has an oriel window and a magnificent ceiling.

Although houses now surround it, Bramhall Hall stands on a green hill overlooking a feeder stream to the Mersey. The view sets the visitor wondering what sort of a river the Mersey once was, is now, and may be

Canoeists on the River Mersey near Sale Water Park.

in the future? These are precisely the questions being asked by those involved in the Mersey Valley project.

On 16th March, 1984, the Department of the Environment issued a long press notice which is worth quoting in full:

Mersey Clean-up Initiative Moves to Third Stage

Patrick Jenkin, Secretary of State for the Environment, announced today that he is establishing a campaign organisation to carry forward the Mersey Clean-up Initiative. Speaking at a Press Conference in Manchester, he said:

"The River Mersey and its tributaries are among the most polluted rivers in Europe. Over the years, the life of the region has turned its back on this great river system. It could be one of the region's finest assets; it has become one of its greatest liabilities.

Michael Heseltine saw this as a great new opportunity. We need to clean up the quality of the water. We need new waterside development schemes. We need new recreational and amenity projects. The river system—its tributaries, its main watercourses and the Mersey estuary itself—should become a focus for the towns and countryside through which they pass.

There is a huge job to be done before we can enjoy a full network of attractive riverside walks, past handsome waterfront buildings and landscaped open spaces; before we can count canoes and sailing dinghies using these waters freely; and watch kingfishers over rivers long deserted by wildlife.

Modern industry and polluted rivers do not go well together. Raw, untreated sewage is a smelly neighbour. Water skiing lacks some of its attraction if the skier's equipment has to include a stomach pump.

In 1982 Michael Heseltine published *Cleaning Up the Mersey*. This went to a wide range of local people and organisations for consultation. Last year Tom King chaired the Mersey Conference at Daresbury. Over 200 people attended the conference and heard speakers from the Water Authority, from the local authorities and from many other bodies.

The enthusiasm was high but it was also realistic. Yes, we face a long difficult haul. Yes, it will require resources—money, people and commitment. And yes, there are arguments about the pace of the programme.

But three clear messages emerged. We need a radical clean-up campaign. We need a new non-statutory body to run it. And we need the Department of the Environment to take the lead.

Last Autumn the North West Water Authority—who have the key role to play—published their own consultation paper on water quality, setting the Mersey Initiative against the needs of the whole region. And only last month the tenth report of the Royal Commission on Environmental Pollution gave firm backing to the Initiative.

We must now move forward. Today I am announcing the establishment of a campaign organisation.

This will be a non-statutory body with three component parts. We want to involve as many groups and organisations as possible. Therefore we will set up a Representative Conference headed by an independent chairman from the region, whom I intend to invite to take the lead. I am already consulting on possible names. The conference would meet, I envisage, in full session every one or two years; would receive progress reports; and it would maintain the momentum of the clean-up campaign.

The direction of the campaign would be in the hands of a board of professional officers under the chairmanship of the DOE regional director. David Renshaw will thus become the first Chairman of the Board. He will be supported by a small but strong team in the DOE regional office, which I hope will include people seconded from outside the Department to bring particular skills and expertise.

And then there will be three project groups to cover the three main divisions of the Mersey basin: the estuary; mid-Mersey and southern; and the upper catchment. These project groups will be built, as far as possible, on existing teams.

The actual work will be done by a wide range of bodies and people; public sector and private sector, statutory and non-statutory, commercial firms, voluntary bodies and local groups of enthusiasts. Obviously the local authorities will play a leading part, as will the North West Water Authority. So I hope will the Countryside Commission and the Sports Council.

Where will the money come from?

At the heart of the campaign will be investment in water quality. Much the greater part of this must come from the North West Water Authority, and that is why their Chairman, George Mann, is on the platform here with me today. The Authority's £170m programme to improve the Mersey Estuary is already well under way. Their strategy document proposed spending £3,700m over 25 years in water quality improvement throughout the North West; the government supports the Authority's long term aims in principle. We shall give the Authority a high priority when allocating external finance with a strong, but certainly not exclusive, concentration on the Mersey basin. Higher standards must inevitably mean higher charges—there is no escaping this. But it is not part of our policy to impose unacceptable costs on the Authority's customers. There is a trade-off between the pace of change and the increase in charges.

The private sector, too, must work in partnership with the Water Authority. An excellent start is the 50 per cent contribution which Shell are making to the extension of the Ellesmere Port Sewage Treatment Works.

Then there is what happens on land. Improved water quality will increase the opportunities and incentives for waterside redevelopment and improvement schemes. Private companies, voluntary bodies, local authorities, the Countryside Commission, the Sports Council all have a role to play. The Department can help with derelict land grants and with the Urban Programme. In making grants I shall want to give priority wherever possible to projects which contribute to the clean-up campaign.

We can look for help from the European Community. Already Community funds are supporting the water authorities' sewage treatment programmes in the Assisted Areas. The European Commission has shown a great interest in the Mersey clean-up campaign and the Government will fight hard for the greatest possible commitment from the European Regional Development Fund.

Next question: how long will it take?

The answer—certainly not less than 25 years. The scale of the problem is enormous. We are coming to grips with more than two centuries of dereliction and pollution. I liken the task to that of the great medieval architects who set out to build the cathedrals which they themselves would never see finished, but which are part of the glory of Britain today.

We must think long and we must think big. The prize is beyond price. It means new jobs, particularly in the construction industry. It is also a new opportunity to harness the commitment of the young to the improvement of our environment; it is a chance to get clean water, pleasant surroundings and new opportunities for leisure. Where there is today squalor and stench, we can bring back the beauty and refreshment of nature.

The time to act is now.

As I pointed out in the introduction, the Mersey and its tributaries are in need of a clean-up, and some may feel that the period of twenty-five years proposed by the authorities could be reduced by a more generous injection of cash and more stringently applied anti-pollution laws. There are a lot of people living around Manchester, however, and the key to success must lie with the North West Water Authority; how quickly can they develop new sewage treatment plants?

The effort to clean up the Mersey Valley was not, in fact, initiated by the central government but by a committee drawn from Stockport,

Manchester, Trafford, the North West Water Authority and the Greater Manchester Council. The Mersey valley has been subject to flooding, a fact well known to the Saxons as well as to their modern counterparts. This has meant that the small villages usually sited on hills could not be industrialised by building factories in the hollows between them. These low-lying areas therefore tended to be used as unsightly dumping grounds, although some oases of rich farmland still exist between them. Road and rail systems sliced across them, and today we are left with an untidy sprawl. It is this which has been the subject of the Mersey Valley Project, which had its origins way back in 1967. We should not look for failures but for the successes, which are not hard to find. Trees have been planted, nature trails set up complete with toilet blocks, snack bars, information centres and full-time wardens.

The rest of this chapter will follow the course of the Mersey from Stockport to the Manchester Ship Canal, which is all part of the Mersey Valley Project. This will take us through a complexity of housing, including Cheadle, Didsbury, Chorlton, Sale, Ashton-on-Mersey, Urmston and Flixton, all villages which have been swallowed by Manchester,

One of the failures along the Mersey, sheet piling at Urmston which was to have provided a barrier against erosion. There have been successes as well.

but for those with "time to stop and stare" they have retained many reminders of their rural origins.

A mere seven miles from Manchester, surrounded and sliced in half by trunk roads, Cheadle has not retained much evidence of its ancient origins except its name. There was a Roman settlement there, and the Saxons set up a cross dedicated to St Chad on the banks of the Mersey. The name is derived from that of the saint and the village was large enough to warrant entry in the Domesday Book.

The church which dominates the busiest part of Cheadle is not the town's original place of worship. Although a building was present around 1200 it was destroyed by fire in 1520, and the replacement church has its share of grinning gargoyles dating from the sixteenth and seventeenth centuries. A sundial has been scratched on the porch, and inside the church itself are some interesting insights into local history. There are two chapels, that to the south having delicate stained glass through which the sun throws a mottled beam on to three stone effigies. These depict Sir John Honford, identified by the lion at his feet, his son-in-law Sir John Stanley, who is bareheaded, and Sir Thomas Brereton. The chapel ought to have had a fourth set of bones, but the body of Sir Thomas Brereton's father, who did so much for the Roundhead cause in Cheshire, is believed to have been lost in the Mersey when floodwaters overwhelmed the coffin as it was being carried across the river. The north chapel with its magnificent sixteenth century screen invites us to pray for the souls of John Savage and his wife.

Also surrounded by modern buildings and traffic is Old Moseley Hall, built in 1666, the year of the fire of London. The building is not in a very good state of repair, and some effort will be needed if the original fireplace and staircase are to survive.

To recreate the atmosphere of the old village of Didsbury, sit in the flowery splendour of the churchyard and listen to the birds singing. The church was rebuilt in 1620 and the pinnacled tower is inscribed with the initials of Sir Edward Mosley, who financed the impressive building. Inside is an alabaster and marble memorial to another member of the family, Sir Nicholas Mosley, onetime Lord Mayor of London. The sculpture shows him in his red robes of office, accompanied by his two wives both sombrely dressed in black. Two of his sons are shown in a much more colourful mood, with red stockings tied with large rosettes, their necks frilled with Elizabethan ruffs. In one wild corner of the churchyard I found a few blooms of wild arum, also known as cuckoo pint, lords and ladies, and very appropriately as starchwort. This plant has a link with the ruffs, since its roots were dug up to produce the starch with which they were stiffened.

The onetime parsonage opposite the church became the home of Fletcher Moss, who made a lifetime's study of old buildings and published seven volumes of *Pilgrimages to Old Houses*. He obviously loved his own historic dwelling, and left it in his will to the citizens of Manchester as a museum. He also left some nearby land, now used as playing fields.

At Chorlton the first visibly effective contribution to the Mersey Valley Project can be seen. Chorlton Water Park is a commendable example of what can be done when working industrialists and realistic conservationists get together. During the construction of the M63 motorway large volumes of easily transportable gravel were needed, and this was extracted at Chorlton and at Sale, both sites being close to the Mersey. The problem of what to do with the unsightly holes was solved by the creation of water parks.

A well-signed road leads from the centre of Chorlton to the car parks and information centres. A footpath which leads around the ponds is lined with native plants such as alder, broom, gorse, birch and oak, and herbs such as lesser celandine and coltsfoot add splashes of delightful colour. Linnets, reed buntings and yellowhammers sing from the treetops and the spikes of bulrushes which grow in the shallows provide

A wintry sky hangs over the Mersey at Chorlton, Manchester, on a January day; there is ice on the riverside footpath.

A fine growth of fungus on a fallen tree beside the Mersey at *Jackson's Boat*, Sale.

ideal cover for the waterfowl. Mallard and tufted duck both breed, and in winter they are joined by other wildfowl, including swans and ducks such as goldeneye and pochard. The great crested grebe also breeds here; it is only because of projects such as the water parks that this lovely species has been brought back from the edge of extinction to its present healthy position. It has been estimated that in 1860 there were only about forty pairs, but at the present time there may be in excess of 6,000 pairs. Both moorhens and coots breed at Chorlton Water Park, where during the spring of 1984 I watched a coot building its nest from discarded crisp packets. On the Ordnance Survey map the area is marked "Chorlton Eyes", eye being the old word for a water meadow, another indication that the Mersey often overflowed its banks.

From the water park a series of steps lead up to the raised banks of the Mersey, which has been rather unsympathetically canalised to prevent flooding. The footpath which leads along the riverbank to Sale is devoid of trees, apparently for the same reason. This is therefore one of the least attractive stretches of the Mersey and I believe would benefit from tree and shrub planting without any risk of flooding. Between Chorlton and *Jackson's Boat* I identified a number of bird-sown plants, including goatsbeard and rosebay willow herb, on which I found in August, 1984, caterpillars of the elephant hawk moth. Pineapple weed and greater plantain were also common, their tough, rough and sticky seeds being easily carried on the soles of shoes and in the treads of bicycle tyres. *Jackson's Boat* is the name of an inn near which an iron footbridge spans the Mersey. The inn sign shows a substantial vessel, but the original ferry would have been a small rowing boat. A footpath from the bridge leads to Chorlton-cum-Hardy, while on the inn side of the river lies Sale. The student of the Mersey, however, should continue on the river bank to Sale Water Park.

An impressive information centre, windsurfers and yachts skimming along under the shadow of the M63, and splendid views over reed beds ensure that Sale Water Park will be popular with visitors. Part of the adjacent Mersey has been accelerated by means of a weir to produce enough white water to encourage a regular flotilla of canoes. The wardens have the assistance of a computer to control the flood of eager visitors.

The only blot on the horizon is a derelict building in the centre of the traffic island serving the link road off the motorway. All that remains of Sale Hall, demolished when the road was built, this is a splendid half timbered dovecote which deserves better treatment than it has been given. Most of the visitors and some of the wardens do not even know what it was. In medieval times, when fodder for cattle could not be kept over winter, there was a huge feast in the autumn followed by a shortage of fresh meat until the breeding cows had given birth the following year. This is where the dovecote came into its own, why they were functional as well as decorative, and why every effort should be made to preserve those which are left.

At Sale the Bridgewater Canal crosses the Mersey. The old town once had an important priory, but today there are gardens on the site. Students of physics will know the importance of the work of James Prescott Joule, who worked out the relationship between heat, work and electrical energy and is buried in Brooklands cemetery, Sale. In the park there is a bust to his memory, the house in which he lived is preserved and there is a plaque on the wall of the Town Hall commemorating his discovery. Born in Salford, Joule studied in Manchester under the celebrated John Dalton, postulator of the Atomic Theory.

From Sale the Mersey, after being joined by Chorlton Brook, winds its way through Ashton-on-Mersey. In these heavily populated areas the sewage outfalls can be a problem after heavy rain, the toxic effluent preventing wild life from gaining a foothold. This is one area which will take time and money to improve.

As the river approaches Flixton and Urmston it has formed an ox-bow system which is surprisingly rich in wildlife and very attractive to look at, despite the river bed being very dirty looking at times.

Before the construction of the Manchester Ship Canal in the 1890s the River Irwell flowed through Manchester and then meandered through the countryside around Trafford Park, Barton and Davyhulme, merging its waters with those of the Mersey a little to the south of Flixton. Both rivers had been made navigable to light traffic as early as the eighteenth century and a number of locks were constructed during the nineteenth. Once the ship canal was finished parts of the Irwell were filled in, although a few stretches of the old course still hold water. There was once a ferry across the Irwell between Flixton and Irlam, and the landing stages can still be seen. A half-mile section near the *Boat House Inn* is now a popular "pond" for anglers, and its banks are a botanist's delight. The re-routing of the Irwell will be described in chapter three.

In the old days Flixton occupied a strategically important spot between the two rivers. St Michael's church was already in existence in 1190, but was substantially re-designed in the eighteenth century and was provided with a stained glass window showing St George and the Dragon. An Elizabethan brass plate depicts Richard Radcliffe, his two wives and a number of their children. A much less pretentious stone records the simple life of a village blacksmith in the words

> My coals are done my debt is paid
> My vices in the dust are laid.

Looking at old maps, it can be seen that Flixton has been called Flixstone, Fluxton and, perhaps significantly, Fleece-Town. An area of the village, the property of the Valentine family, was known as Shaw, the family seat being Shaw Hall, unfortunately demolished in 1955. Shaw Hall Avenue and Shaw Hall Crescent mark the site of the hall. I wonder if the residents ever see the ghost of Sir Ralph Valentine, who was killed with many of his retainers at the battle of Bosworth in 1485 when Henry Tudor defeated Richard III. Sir Ralph's wife had a premonition of his death, and several folk said they had seen his heavily armoured ghost riding from the direction of the Mersey. Apart from Shaw Hall Avenue and Shaw Hall Crescent, the only reminder we have of Shaw Hall is a number of Jacobean oak panels which survived the demolition and were removed to Flixton House.

Flixton House was the home of the Wright family, who turned out to be wrong! Judge Ralph Wright enlarged his seventeenth century farmhouse in 1806 and later blocked a public right of way in order to enlarge his private estate. The Association for the Preservation of Ancient Footpaths was formed in 1826 and in a test case the following

Sale Water Park,
Cheshire;
sailboarding
under the
shadow of the
M63.

year the locals won; all of us who love the countryside have cause to bless the walkers of Flixton. The last of the family, the bachelor Samuel Worthington Wright, died in 1934. Flixton house was bought by the urban district council and the historic and pleasantly airy house is now open for lectures and other social functions.

Urmston has gone one better than its neighbour Flixton by demolishing both of its halls. Urmston Hall was demolished in 1937 to make room for the estate houses of Manor Avenue; Newcroft Hall went in 1935, to be replaced by another estate comprising Newcroft Road, Crescent and Drive.

The word Urmston comes from Ormes Tun, which means the dwelling of Orme, who was the son of Edward Aylward. He was given a caracute of land in the early thirteenth century as a dowry when he married Emma, the daughter of Albert de Grelly. A caracute was a somewhat haphazard unit of area, being defined as the total land which a team of oxen could plough in a year. The de Grelly family had obtained their lands close to the Mersey by the grace of Roger de Poictou, a supporter of William of Normandy whose loyalty to his king brought him the reward of substantial tracts of land between the Ribble and the Mersey. Some of Urmston's old cottages do remain, but no matter how many are demolished one former resident of Urmston will not be forgotten as long as dialect writing gives us joy. This is the remarkable John Collier, who wrote under the name of Tim Bobbin and was the first person ever to write in the Lancashire dialect, or "Lanky twang" as the locals call it. He has been called the "Burns of Lancashire", and his *Tummas and Meary* is arguably the best dialect story ever written. John Collier was the third son of Urmston's curate and schoolmaster.

Describing his own childhood, "Tim Bobbin" wrote, using the third person:

> In the reign of Queen Anne he was a boy and one of the nine children of a poor curate in Lancashire, whose stipend never amounted to thirty pounds a year, and consequently the family must feel the iron teeth of penury with a witness. These indeed were sometimes blunted by the charitable disposition of the good rector (The Rev. Mr. Haddon of Wigton). So this T.B. lived as some other boys did, content with water porridge, buttermilk and jannock, till he was between thirteen and fourteen years of age when Providence began to smile on him on his advancement to a pair of Dutch looms, when he met with treacle to his pottage, and sometimes a little in his buttermilk or spread on his jannock. However, the reflection of his father's circumstances (which now and then start up and still edge his teeth) make him believe that Pluralists are no good Christians.

Pluralism, in which one clergyman took the livings from many churches, but served none, was indeed one of the scourges of the age. Instead he employed curates on starvation wages to do the work. It is small wonder that the hungry Urmston urchin watched his father, blind and hungry, struggling to feed his family. The writings of Tim Bobbin show a hatred of the Church which his father had intended him to enter. Lack of money prevented him making the Church his career. Instead he was apprenticed to a weaver in Mottram in 1732, but he wandered the moors in his spare time and eventually set himself up as a travelling schoolmaster. He did very well teaching in Milnrow, near Rochdale, and also earned money from his writing and by painting inn signs. His fondness for ale meant that his own large family sometimes went short, but he lived to the ripe old age of seventy-six, dying in 1786. He is buried with his wife in the churchyard at Rochdale.

I like to think of young John Collier chasing butterflies and picking flowers along Urmston and Flixton ees, the water meadows of the Mersey. Perhaps he stood on Carrington bridge and looked at the farms at Carrington, where the power station and chemical complexes now stand. On his way to Rochdale he must have walked down Boat Lane to Irlam Ferry. Some of these old roads can still be followed, but the Mersey does not now merge with the Irwell but with the Manchester Ship Canal opposite the ruins of the Irlam steelworks. The Mersey and the ship canal then run together until Bollin Point, when the river swings away from the canal and winds its way into Warrington.

Assorted debris gathers at the foot of the weir and detergent foam provides evidence of pollution as the River Mersey tumbles into the Manchester Ship Canal at Irlam Weir.

CHAPTER THREE

The Dark River—The Irwell

N O RIVER is so consistently maligned as the Irwell unless it be its tributaries the Roch, Croal, Irk and Medlock; music hall jokes about falling in and being dissolved rather than drowned are still the stock-in-trade of clubland's comics. It is also said that the Irwell flows through some of the most industrialised and most impoverished areas in Britain.

Are these accusations true? There is seldom smoke without fire and though as a whole things are improving—very rapidly in some areas—the poor old Irwell certainly still has its problems. I do, however, live close to it and object to its being painted all black, for it has areas of great beauty and it was, after all, its waters which turned the first cogs to drive the wheel of the Industrial Revolution on which the wealth of our nation was firmly based.

There are two possible derivations of the name. It could come from the Anglo-Saxon "Ere-Well", meaning the white spring, or more likely from Irr-well, meaning dark river (probably due to its peaty constituents).

Deerplay moor, where the Irwell has its birth, lies 1,454 feet above Bacup and is only twenty feet lower than the nearby ancient beacon point of Thievely Pike. The deer which traditionally played here have gone, although a red deer was run over on the moor in April, 1984. Wheatears, short-eared owls, merlins and twite make the area popular with bird-watchers. Plants such as bog asphodel, cotton grass, ragged robin, butterwort and heather give the botanist an excuse to fill the lungs when wandering these windy hills. The presence of the magnificent emperor moth adds splendour and colour to the scene.

The source of the river is easy to find since it is so close to the A671 in the fields of Irwell Farm, then trickling off towards and around the premises of the equally well-named Irwell Springs Printing Company which began work in 1813 but has been closed for many years. The tiny rivulet soon picks up other streams and descends steeply into a narrow damp valley in which lies Bacup, the first of the Irwell's many cotton towns. Before it arrives in Bacup it is already tainted with iron oxide from the disused mines of Old Deerplay and the unusual Old Meadows mine in which coal was obtained by the pillar-and-stall method. The coal was shovelled into bogeys which were pushed along a narrow gauge railway out of the pit and downhill towards Bacup. The mine was still working as late as 1969; it is a pity that efforts made to preserve it as a "semi-working museum" failed. There is, however, a wealth of old mining material available in the museum of Bacup Natural History Society, situated near to the town centre. The "Bacup Nats'" museum is, indeed, one of the most pleasant and informative centres in this grand old mill town. Here you may learn about the history of the town, its industries, churches and chapels, and inspect a most fascinating collection of local bugs, butterflies and birds. You will be invited to drink tea and have your leg pulled.

The museum was founded in the 1870s by a knowledgeable group of artisan naturalists who learned latin names for plants by propping their flora against their looms. By hard work they acquired, and still maintain, their own rooms in which are a mass of exhibits varying from miners' helmets to mallards, looms to lapwings, a gas lamp to a goshawk. Ancient washing machines rub shoulders with a First World War packet of Woodbines—the whole place has a lived-in look, so often absent from clinically organised "thou shalt not touch" modern museums. The library is magnificent—and the books are read; it includes a lovely seventeenth

The Britannia Coconut Dancers performing in the streets of Bacup, keeping up a tradition which possibly originated in the Middle East and was brought back by the Crusaders. *Lancashire Evening Telegraph*

century copy of Camden's *Britannia*. Copies of old newspapers are filed away along with ancient maps of the Irwell.

The town is justly proud of the magnificent moors which surround it and sad at the closure of the great majority of its cotton mills and associated bleach and fabric printing works which kept local coffers full and confidence high. Every Easter Saturday, however, the town takes on a carnival atmosphere as crowds gather to watch the team of Britannia Coconut Dancers performing all day along the main street, which stretches from the *Britannia* at one end to the *Irwell Inn* at the other. At this point the Irwell is confined between high concrete barriers, a precaution against flooding, but its waters now usually look clean and benches by the riverside make for pleasant sitting, especially when fortified by a pint of beer and listening to the impulsive rhythm of the dance.

The group consists of musicians plus a team of eight colourful, muscular, male dancers, their faces blackened to resemble Moors. These were probably known to the Crusaders of the eleventh and twelfth centuries, who may well have brought the dance tradition back from the Middle East. Indeed it may well be that the old name for troupes like these was Moorish and not Morris dancers. The "Bacup moors" are driven on by a "Whiffler" with an ornate stick; the dancers keep time with

Left: The Irwell under Burnley Road, Bacup.

Opposite: Culverting the Irwell at Bacup in 1912.
Bacup Natural History Society

their polished clogs, bells and with blocks of wood, looking like coconut shells, which are fastened to their hands, feet and knees.

Whenever I visit Bacup and follow the Irwell I can always imagine the rhythm of the coconut men; the hard-working river seems to shake off its industrial image, sparkle in the sunlight and dance with them. On its five-mile journey to Rawtenstall the Irwell is topped up by a number of smaller streams at Stacksteads, while Cowpe Brook and Whitewell Brook join the growing river at the well named Waterfoot. Both these streams have several pairs of resident dippers, and kingfishers once more flash like an electric spark under their bridges. A few years ago this would have been unheard of, but with the loss of cotton and especially bleaching mills the streams can once more support invertebrates and the fish, including trout, which depend upon them.

Another town whose damp valley made it ideal for cotton spinning, Rawtenstall is still a bottleneck for traffic between Manchester and Burnley, in spite of being linked by a dual carriageway with the M62. The birch-lined valleys (locally known as cloughs) around the town ensure that the countryside is never far from the bustle of the town, whose history and natural history is faithfully and attractively recorded in the Whittaker Park Museum and Art Gallery. Apart from a rather incongruous shrunken head, there are interesting local features including a

Flood damage in St James Street, Bacup, caused by the River Irwell in 1950.
Bacup Natural History Society

display of the art of clog making and an impressive collection of toll boards removed from the turnpike highways of the district. There were important salt roads and lime roads, carrying essential limestone from the Ribblesdale area, running through the villages of Rossendale, of which Rawtenstall is one.

On the Burnley side of Rawtenstall is the much older village of Crawshawbooth, from which the well-named Limey Water trickles down to join the Irwell. Parts of the village show the impact of the Industrial Revolution, when mills poured bleach into the stream and soot into the atmosphere and played their notes into the death symphony of the Irwell. It was, however, an important settlement in the old hunting forest of Rossendale and its oldest house is Swinshaw Hall, which some workers feel may have played a part in the destruction of the last wild boar in England. *Sir Gawain and the Green Knight*, a story set in the late fourteenth century, tells the gory tale of this last great hunt; the work contains a great deal of northern dialect. Some authorities set the action in Wildboarclough way up in Goyt and Bollin country, while others favour Crawshawbooth. Apart from its impressive church of St John, with Limey Water trickling past its tree-lined churchyard, Crawshawbooth was once home to those who did not conform to the Anglican doctrine. Goodshaw chapel is an early example of a Baptist building constructed in 1760, while on the banks of Limey Water close to an old packhorse bridge is a Quaker meeting house built in 1716 and possessing a chair in which George Fox, founder of the sect, once sat. At the rear of the meeting house are stables where the brethren, who often travelled many miles to pray in a safe house, could rest their horses. The track which leads from the packhorse bridge over the moors passes a locally popular animal sanctuary and graveyard where those who wish to remember their dog, cat, budgie or even alligator can have it interred with dignity, the grave capped with a memorial stone.

Compared to such history Rawtenstall is somewhat modern and mundane, but St Mary's is a lovely church with its symmetrical turret topped with a tiny spire peeping out between a belt of trees and its bells answered by passing rooks. High above the town is Waugh's Well, named after a writer who lived in the late nineteenth century and produced a flood of poems and prose in the true dialect tradition of Tim Bobbin and Ammon Wrigley. It is known that the great man loved to rest here, drink of the cool, clear water and listen to the song of the soaring lark.

From Rawtenstall the Irwell flows south-west, more or less following the A681, and on its way to Ramsbottom absorbs the substantial flow of water from the River Ogden. In former years the Irwell was much more liable to flood, but it is now pretty well managed along most of its course. Just before reaching Ramsbottom the river plunges down towards the industrial village of Stubbins, which is sometimes flooded after heavy rain or when snow is melting off the moors, cutting the road link from Bolton to Burnley. Usually, however, the Irwell is well behaved and rolls gently into Ramsbottom.

The name of the town is said to relate to its function as a gathering ground for sheep, but some have suggested that Ramsbottom comes from HRAMSA, the Old English word for wild garlic, which today we still call ramsons. This pungently smelling plant with its deep green leaves and pure white flowers still grows in the damp valley of the Irwell below the town. Before the Industrial Revolution Ramsbottom was just a farming village set between two hills fringed with trees and flushed by gurgling ice-cool streams plunging down to the trout-full Irwell. On both hills there is now a monument to the mighty men of Victorian England. On one stands a tower commemorating the industrious lives of the Grant brothers and on the other is a similar monument to Robert Peel.

Never were two brothers more devoted than William and Charles Grant, who were immortalised by Charles Dickens as the Cheeryble brothers in *Nicholas Nickleby*. Born in Inverness of farming stock, but robbed of their inheritance by an horrendous flood, they came south and found jobs in a print works near Bury. Their ambition was to set up business on their own; the question was where? They eventually decided upon Ramsbottom, some say by climbing a local hill and tossing a pointed stick into the air to see which way fate pointed. They worked hard and honestly, eventually making a million pounds—no mean feat at any time, but especially in Victorian England. The Grants never lost the common touch, were generous with their time and their money, and deserve their monument more than most. There are other monuments to them appropriately in the church of St Andrew's which stands above the valley. Inside is a fine bust of William and a clock with a twenty-nine-foot pendulum, one of the longest in the country. St Paul's Church with its elegant spire and stained glass lords it over the River Irwell.

The monument on Holcombe Hill commemorates the busy life of Sir Robert Peel, whose good deeds were national rather than parochial in nature. The Peel family originated in Blackburn but made their money from calico printing in the Bury area. Following in his father's footsteps, Robert went to Westminster in 1809 and in 1822 became Home Secretary, a post in which he excelled; he was responsible for the setting up of the Metropolitan Police in 1829. The constables became known as "Peelers" or "Bobbies" after the founder of their force. By 1834 Peel was Prime Minister, but he resigned in 1835, only to take up the reigns again in 1841. Apart from being active in the repeal of the Corn Laws, Peel did much to improve the lot of the workers in his native Lancashire and well deserves his hillside spot. The Peel monument has a stone staircase leading to the top, from which there are spectacular views over the whole valley. It was built in 1851 at a cost of £1,000 which was raised by public subscription and to which the Grant brothers contributed.

After Ramsbottom the course of the river is more or less due south, picking up Holcombe Brook (running through a village which still has a foxhunt) and Kirklees Brook, which drains Tottington, before skirting Bury and entering Radcliffe where it is joined by the River Roch.

The bulk of the town of Radcliffe was built during the Industrial Revolution, but as far back as Anglo-Saxon times the hill of red sandstone above the Irwell was settled. The old name was Rate-Clive, meaning the red cliff. The Normans tried to rename it Rougemont, but the Saxons hereabouts were stubborn—they still are—and the old name remains. The Radcliffe family dominated the Bury area for almost 500 years and "William Radcliffe of the Tower" was called to the Grand Inquest of the County of Lancaster in the year 1211. The remains of the Radcliffe tower now lie in ruins and the extensive deer park is buried under a concrete jungle. It was politics which made the family, and politics which destroyed them. One Radcliffe took the side of John the Regent against

Richard the Lionheart, for which indiscretion he was luckily only fined. By 1403 they were back on the right side, because Henry IV readily gave James de Radcliffe permission "to embattle and fortify" his house on the Irwell. By the time of Richard III, however, the family were back once more on the wrong side of the political blanket and in his play Shakespeare records the event for posterity. We should remember, however, that the playwright lived in Tudor England and therefore did not support Richard III.

> The Catte, the Ratte and Lovel our dog
> Ruleth all England under a Hogge

In this Shakespeare refers to Catesby as a cat (Guy Fawkes, living in the next century, was a Catesby and related to the Radcliffes at Odsall Hall in Salford) and the Ratte was of course Radcliffe himself; Lord Lovel had a dog on his family crest and poor old Richard III of the Plantagenet line was shown as a pig, which must have delighted Shakespeare's monarch. Throughout the play Radcliffe has a prominent role, which underlines how highly the family were regarded by the King.

The Pits—pollution and refuse on the River Roch at Rochdale.

They recovered from Bosworth and as a result of a series of sensible marriages a Radcliffe became Earl of Sussex in the reign of Henry VIII and another the Earl of Derwentwater when he married an illegitimate daughter of Charles II in 1688. The fateful family became extinct probably because of the pro-Stuart rebellions of 1715 and 1745, when more than one head was laid before the executioner's axe. The Radcliffes have left one true reminder in the form of an alabaster tombstone in the church showing a knight and his lady. They have also left one untrue tale of a jealous step-mother ridding herself of her husband's only daughter by having her killed and baked in a pie. A faithful page-boy failed to save the lass

> Oh save her life good master cook
> And make your pies of me
> For pity's sake do not destroy
> My lady with your knife
> You know she is your father's joy
> For Christ's sake save her life.

Ellen of Radcliffe is thus done to death, but her enemies did not escape.

> Then all in black this lord did mourne
> And for his daughter's sake
> He judged her cruell stepmother
> To be burnt at the stake
>
> Likewise he judged the master cook
> In boiling lead to stand;
> And made the simple scullion boy
> The heir to all his land.

Otters were once present on the Mersey and its tributaries until pollution killed the fish on which they fed. Will they ever return?

At the time of the Radcliffes the Irwell abounded with fish, and it seems strange to relate that one of the greatest otter hunts took place on a stretch of the Irwell between Prestwich and Radcliffe. A poem of the time records the hunt from the otter's point of view

I am a brave otter, as you shall hear,
I've rambled the country all round;
I valued no dogs far or near,
In the water nor yet on the ground.

I valued no dogs far or near,
But I roved through the country so wide,
Til I came to a river so clear,
That did Clifton and Prestwich divide.

And through the wild country I rambled,
I liv'd at extravagant rate
On eels, chubs and gudgeons I feasted;
The fishermen all did me hate.

Yet still up the river I went,
Where the fishes my stomach did cheer.
Till a challenge from Radcliffe they sent me,
They quickly would stop my career.

Soon after this poem was popular, industry drove both fishes and otters from the Mersey and its tributaries, but two otters were killed near Bowdon on the River Bollin in 1849. Although Radcliffe is a busy town a quiet sit by the river, now swelled by the sometimes mucky waters of the Roch, still evokes memories of the beautiful Ellen and her step-mother, boiling lead, Jacobite insurrections, Tudor squabbles, the Wars of the Roses and other events played out under the red sandstone cliffs overlooking the Irwell.

Between Radcliffe and Farnworth the Irwell has been disturbed by weirs and bridged by canals and railways constructed to transport the products of cotton and paper industries. Mills also sprang up along the River Croal, which powered many waterwheels in the early days of Bolton's growth. Rock Hall (also known as Moses Gate Country Park) is the centre of one of Greater Manchester's River Valley Projects, this one based on the Croal and Irwell.

Rock Hall itself is located near the A6053 and was the home of the Crompton family, who developed a revolutionary and cheap method of making both paper and their own fortune. Their deserted house had become almost derelict but since 1977 has been restored, with lecture facilities and a book shop. It was not just papermaking which blighted this lovely riverscape but also fabric printing, coal mining and chemical manufacture. Around Rock Hall native trees have been planted, orchids bloom in the damp areas and butterflies such as blues, whites and meadow browns are abundant. Archeological interests are also considered and the Manchester to Bolton Canal, especially at nearby Prestolee, provides a spectacular example of hydro-engineering. The work of the valley scheme continues and at the time of writing sixteen areas are being actively improved along the Irwell itself and on the Croal and its two main tributaries, the Bradshaw Brook and the River Tonge.

The Irwell now heads off through Carr Clough, looping around what was one of Manchester's golf courses and lapping the now defunct racecourse. It is soon joined by the Irk and eventually by the Medlock. Few rivers divide two cities as does the Irwell, with Salford on one bank and Manchester on the other. There is no space here to cover the history of this area in detail and the reader is referred to the bibliography.

Even before the construction of the ship canal great efforts had been made to make the Irwell and the Mersey navigable at least to small ships. The history of these efforts is well documented by John Corbridge in his excellent *Pictorial History of the Mersey and Irwell Navigation*. The Irwell used to meet the Mersey at Flixton but now drains into Manchester docks, at the top end of the ship canal. Two fascinating quotes illustrate the ups and downs of the Irwell. In J. Corbett's book *The River Irwell*, written in 1907, we are given a graphic account of the river around 1837, the year Queen Victoria began her reign.

> Standing, in 1907, at Hunts Bank, now called Victoria Street, in front of the Manchester Cathedral, let us imagine the view down the river some seventy years ago. Instead of the present wide roadway, with its iron railings along the river wall, we should see a closely packed mass of buildings of very poor quality, with narrow pathways between them, and several flights of steps partly cut in the red sandstone rock of the steep river bank, by which the people carried up water from the river for various domestic purposes; there being as yet no adequate waterworks for the town.
>
> Instead of Victoria Bridge there was the ancient and picturesque Salford Bridge. The original bridge on this site was the first bridge across the Irwell; it was a wooden structure, erected about the year 1365. The will of Thomas de Bothe, 1368, provides for building a chapel upon the Salford Bridge, "where prayers were wont to be made for the repose of the soul of the founder". In 1538 this bridge is recorded as being then of stone in three arches, with "a pretty little chapel". This stone bridge was built with three pointed arches, and projecting angular piers, over which were recesses for the safety of foot passengers when horses and vehicles were crossing; the roadway was originally only about twelve feet wide, and after widening on each side, in two successive improvements, was finally only about twenty-six feet wide. The small chapel was built over the detached pier on the Salford side, on the upstream side of the bridge; and in 1505 this chapel was made into a prison, in which the hymn, "Jerusalem, My Happy Home," was written, apparently by J. Bromehead; but in

Prestolee aqueduct carrying the Manchester, Bury and Bolton Canal over the River Irwell at Prestolee, near Bolton.

1580 a new jail was built on Hunts Bank. In 1776 the old chapel was taken down and the bridge widened. This bridge seems to have been free of tolls.

A temporary wooden footbridge was provided during the last rebuilding operations in 1838, and this was destroyed by a flood in the river. We find many records of injurious floods from that time to this, and even in earlier years before the numerous bridges and the encroaching buildings on the river banks increased the liability to flooding.

When the present bridge, in one clear span of ninety-nine feet, was being built, the first stone on the Manchester side was laid by the Boroughreeve of Salford, Elkanah Armitage, Esq., on March 31st, 1838; and on 2nd July the first stone on the Salford side was laid by the Boroughreeve of Manchester, J. Brown, Esq. On 10th October the arch centres or scaffoldings were washed away by a flood, and considerable damage done to the works; and the centres were blown down by a gale on 7th January, 1839. The keystone of the arch was set by Humphrey Trafford, Esq., on 23rd March, and on 20th June, 1839, the bridge was opened with a grand procession. An engraved panel was fixed outside the north battlement to record its history, and that its erection had cost £20,800. It was named Victoria Bridge in honour of the young Queen, who was very popular even in those first years of her reign.

On the Salford side, just above the bridge, stood the Woollen Cloth Hall, with an open colonnade (now partly walled up) fronting the river; and stone steps down to a sloping gravel bank, also approached from Chapel Street by the still existing narrow road called Stanihurst. On this sloping river bank were a number of rowing boats for hire in "Mary Ann's Boathouse".

It was common practice to drive horses down this bank to drink at the river, or to have their coach wheels washed, and in November, 1798, a gentleman's carriage was so taken by the coachman nearly at midnight; but the river was somewhat in flood, and horses, coach, and man were washed away. The man jumped on a dyer's flat and escaped, the coach and horses got jammed in New Bailey Bridge, and next day eight persons were drowned there by giving way of a projecting wooden shed, from which eleven people were looking at the wrecked coach. One of the three survivors was saved by a dog.

On the Manchester side, just below Victoria Bridge, there was a very busy landing stage, connected in later years with "Ben Lang's Music Hall," where many rowing boats were on hire, and where small steamers started for pleasure trips down the river to Pomona Gardens and other holiday resorts.

By 1844 the effect of industry had really begun to bite and Frederick Engels in his politically biased but in some ways brutally accurate work *The conditions of the working class in England 1844-5* describes the poor condition of the Irwell:

Manchester proper lies on the left bank of the Irwell, between that stream and the two smaller ones, the Irk and the Medlock, which here empty into the Irwell. On the right bank of the Irwell, bounded by a sharp curve of the river, lies Salford, and farther westward Pendleton; northward from the Irwell lie Upper and Lower Broughton; northward of the Irk, Cheetham Hill; south of the Medlock lies Hulme; farther east Chorlton on Medlock; still farther pretty well to the east of Manchester, Ardwick. The whole assemblage of buildings is commonly called Manchester, and contains about four hundred thousand inhabitants, rather more than less. The town itself is peculiarly built, so that a person may live in it for years, and go in and out daily without coming into contact with a working-people's quarter or even with workers, that is, so long as he confines himself to his business or to pleasure walks. This arises chiefly from the fact, that by unconscious tacit agreement, as well as with out-spoken conscious determination, the working-people's quarters are sharply separated from the sections of the city reserved for the middle-class; or, if this does not succeed, they are concealed with the cloak of charity. Manchester contains, at its heart, a rather extended commercial district, perhaps half a mile long and about as broad, and consisting almost wholly of offices and warehouses. Nearly the whole district is abandoned by dwellers, and is lonely and deserted at night, only watchmen and policemen traverse its narrow lanes with their dark lanterns. This district is cut through by certain main thoroughfares upon which the vast traffic concentrates, and in which the ground level is lined with brilliant shops. In these streets the upper floors are occupied, here and there, and there is a good deal of life upon them until late at night. With the exception of this commercial district, all Manchester proper, all Salford and Hulme, a great part of Pendleton and Chorlton, two-thirds of Ardwick, and single stretches of Cheetham Hill and Broughton are all unmixed working-people's quarters, stretching like a girdle, averaging a mile and a half in breadth, around the commercial district. Outside, beyond this girdle, lives the upper and middle bourgeoisie, the middle bourgeoisie in regularly laid out streets in the vicinity of the working quarters, especially in Chorlton and the lower lying portions of Cheetham Hill; the upper bourgeoisie in remoter villas with gardens in Chorlton and Ardwick, or on the breezy heights of Cheetham Hill, Broughton, and Pendleton, in free, wholesome country air, in fine, comfortable homes, passed once every half or quarter hour by omnibuses going into the city. And the finest part of the arrangement is this, that the members of this money aristocracy can take the shortest road through the middle of all the labouring districts to their places of business, without ever seeing that they are in the midst of the grimy misery that lurks to the right and the left....

The south bank of the Irk is .... very steep and between fifteen and thirty feet high. On this declivitous hillside there are planted three rows of houses, of which the lowest rise directly out of the river, while the front walls of the highest stand on the crest of the hill in Long Millgate. Among them are mills on the river, in short, the method of construction is as crowded and disorderly here as in the lower part of Long Millgate. Right and left a multitude of covered passages lead from the main street into numerous courts, and he who turns in thither gets into a filth and disgusting grime, the equal of which is not to be found, especially in the courts which lead down to the Irk, and which contain unqualifiedly the most horrible dwellings which I have yet beheld. In one of these courts there stands directly at the entrance, at the end of the covered passage, a privy without a door, so dirty that the inhabitants can pass into and out of the court only by passing through foul pools of stagnant urine and excrement. This is the first court on the Irk above Ducie Bridge—in case any one should care to look into it. Below it on the river there are several tanneries which fill the whole neighbourhood with the stench of animal putrefaction. Below Ducie Bridge the only entrance to most of the houses is by means of narrow, dirty stairs and over heaps of refuse and filth. The first court below Ducie Bridge, known as Allen's Court, was in such a state at the time of the cholera that the sanitary police ordered it evacuated, swept, and disinfected with chloride of lime. Dr Kay gives a terrible description of the state of this court at that time. Since then, it seems to have been partially torn away and rebuilt; at least looking down from Ducie Bridge, the passer-by sees several ruined walls, and heaps of debris with some newer houses. The view from this bridge, mercifully concealed from mortals of small stature by a

51

parapet as high as a man, is characteristic for the whole district. At the bottom flows, or rather stagnates, the Irk, a narrow, coal-black, foul-smelling stream, full of debris and refuse, which it deposits on the shallower right bank. In dry weather, a long string of the most disgusting, blackish-green, slime pools are left standing on this bank, from the depths of which bubbles of miasmatic gas constantly arise and give forth a stench unendurable even on the bridge forty or fifty feet above the surface of the stream. But besides this, the stream itself is checked every few paces by high weirs, behind which slime and refuse accumulate and rot in thick masses. Above the bridge are tanneries, bone mills, and gasworks, from which all drains and refuse find their way into the Irk, which receives further the contents of all the neighbouring sewers and privies. It may be easily imagined, therefore, what sort of residue the stream deposits. Below the bridge you look upon the piles of debris, the refuse, filth and offal from the courts on the steep left bank; here each house is packed close behind its neighbour and a piece of each is visible, all black, smoky, crumbling, ancient, with broken panes and window-frames. The background is furnished by old barrack-like factory buildings. On the lower right bank stands a long row of houses and mills; the second house being a ruin without a roof, piled with debris; the third stands so low that the lowest floor is un-inhabitable, and therefore without windows or doors. Here the background embraces the pauper burial-ground, the station of the Liverpool and Leeds railway, and in the rear of this, the workhouse, the 'Poor-Law Bastille' of Manchester, which, like a citadel, looks threateningly down from behind its high walls and parapets on the hilltop, upon the working-people's quarter below.

The present condition of the Irwell in Manchester is much better than this gloomy picture. There can be no doubt that it is steadily improving; I have watched tufted duck and goldeneyes gliding around quite happily very close to Deansgate. Many of the old eyesore buildings have gone and there are plans to set up river walks with seats and flower beds. Likewise great strides are being made to clean up the tributaries of the Irwell.

Oh, gentle Roch, my native stream
Oft when a careless boy,
I've prattled to thee in a dream
As thou went singing by.

So wrote Edwin Waugh in 1889 of one of Lancashire's most polluted rivers, but one to which Rochdale must give thanks for past prosperity. Harrison, a geographer writing in the time of Queen Elizabeth I, described the course of the river and in 1946 W.T. Palmer modernised the old description. The Roch, he said, "rises among the black stony hills from whence it goeth to Littleborough and being past Clegg, receiveth the Byle, that cometh hither by Milnrow Chapel. After this confluence also it meeteth with a rill near unto Rochdale, and soon after with the

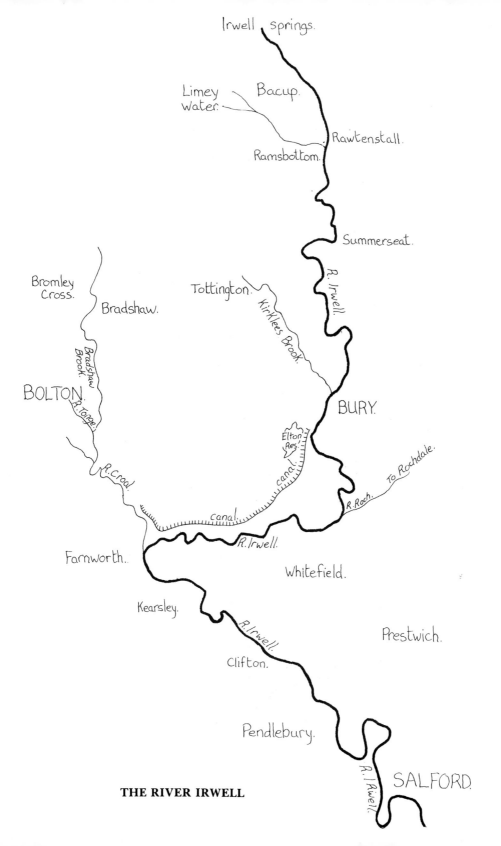

THE RIVER IRWELL

The *Tim Bobbin* inn at Milnrow which commemorates the pen name of schoolmaster John Collier, writer of dialect poetry.

Spodden Water, and then the Sudley Brook, whereby his channel is not a little increased which goeth into the .... Irwell before it cometh to Radcliffe".

Milnrow was the home of John Collier, alias Tim Bobbin, who was employed as schoolmaster from 1739 to his death in 1796. His output of dialect poems was remarkable—it had to be, for he paid for many things, including ale, with a book of his poems which he printed himself. In his diary he records that he "Paid John Kenyon a book for a wig" and on another occasion he "Exchanged a book of *Human Passions* for 3lbs of thread at 3s per lb; blue tape 1/2d a yard tape 1d a knot; a gross of laces".

The Roch is typified by narrow glens through which its waters tumble. Two miles above the town is Tyrone's Bed where it is alleged that an Irish rebel of Elizabethan times, the Earl of Tyrone, hid himself while

A wintry scene on the River Irk at Middleton, with the Lever Bridge at left and Ackrington Hall at the top of the hill.

visiting his lover, Constance Halt, of Grizlehurst. The Spodden also hurtles through a narrow channel of rock known locally as the Thrutch, or more romantically as the Fairies' Chapel. Another tributary is the Naden, which joins the Roch at Hooley Bridge.

Rochdale's original prosperity was based on wool—cotton came later. Its fame is based partly on the first co-operative store set up on Toad Lane in 1844 and partly on its being the birthplace of Gracie Fields. The banks of the River Roch, now culverted under the town centre, once supported a Bronze Age settlement; the museum displays many of the settlers' artefacts. The Romans knew the Roch, as part of their road from Manchester to York passed through and up to Blackstone Edge, where a goodly proportion of it still exists. Rochdale was a West Saxon settlement, warranted a substantial mention in the Domesday Book and was granted its weekly market charter way back in 1251. John Bright the politician was born in Rochdale in 1811 and along with Peel fought hard against the Corn Laws. He is remembered by a bronze statue in Hillside Gardens.

The Irk brings its murky waters from the hills above Middleton down through what must once have been splendid countryside around Cheetham and Harpurhey. Blighted, bridged, channelled, culverted, polluted and diverted, the Irk eventually joins the Irwell around Victoria station. Has the Irk no virtues at all? Yes, it has—Middleton with its attractive church rebuilt in the sixteenth century and the *Boar's Head Inn*, a black and white building dating back to the seventeenth century. It is the church, however, which is the key to the town's history. A stained glass window depicts the archers from Middleton who fought at Flodden field under the command of Sir Ralph Assheton. St Leonard's Church has another interesting feature, a tower with an unusual wooden belfry cap and gables, obviously later, but fascinating additions.

The Medlock rises around Bishop Park to the north-east of Oldham,

Left: Detergent foam on the Roch at Smallbridge, near Rochdale.

Opposite: The River Medlock at Daisy Nook on Easter Monday.

then flows for ten miles separating Oldham and Ashton before entering one of Manchester's urban areas and flowing thence to the Irwell. When local government reorganisation took place in 1974 the new councils got together to talk about the state of the Medlock. Great strides have been made to improve the river valley. Derelict land has been reclaimed, thousands of trees planted, pollution has been halted, if not completely controlled. An impressive country park has been set up at Daisy Nook and wildlife has responded to the improved environment. Visitors have followed and many of the city's children get their first lessons in natural history from either the full-time warden service or from the many local enthusiasts who give freely of their time. Within the Medlock Valley there are splendid parks, facilities for angling, horse riding, boating, walking or just sitting.

It is impossible to write about the Irwell or the Mersey without a feeling for its beauty and the history of its distant past, some sorrow for its immediate past, and without a bounding optimism for its future.

CHAPTER FOUR

The Mersey's Canals

AS MANCHESTER and the district around it grew into Britain's biggest industrial centre the poor old Irwell just could not cope, and the vital link to the port of Liverpool became so overcrowded as to threaten the security of both cities. It is small wonder that the Canal Age began in Manchester, and within a few years a series of cuts ran in all directions from the hub of industry like the spokes of a wheel.

Francis Egerton, later the Duke of Bridgewater, born in 1736, gambled his family fortune on the value of a canal system—and won. His foresight can be appreciated when, at the height of his success, he looked at the crude efforts to build steam engines and said of his canals that "They will last my time, but I see danger in those damned railways". The main feature of the Bridgewater Canal is not, as is often suggested, that it was the first canal to be cut, but that it was the first in England to be completely independent of any existing river course and to have the backing of an Act of Parliament (1759).

The Duke's initial request was for a cut to run from Hollins Green near Irlam on the Mersey, via Worsley, where he had his house and his coal mines, and on to the river Irwell at Salford. There is no doubt, however, that he had his eye on Liverpool. The problem of how to get the coal to the canal was solved by running a cut from Worsley straight into the mines, floating the coal out in barges. This, once the canal was built, substantially reduced the price of coal in Manchester and made the Industrial Revolution in the area a certainty—it had cheap power.

The Duke of Bridgewater not only saw the value of canal transport but he also had an eye for genius; he gave James Brindley the post of consultant engineer—an inspired choice. Prior to Brindley's appointment the Duke's agent, John Gilbert, had done a great deal of accurate planning. The Irwell was in the way of the canal, so Brindley crossed it in 1761 with the Barton Aqueduct, one of the wonders of this or any other age. From a sleepy village in 1750, Worsley suddenly became the industrial centre of the north. These days it has settled down to life as a museum, where visitors come to see the beauty of the old hall, home of the Duke of Bridgewater, reflected in the waters of his canal, often stained red by iron salts from the mines which still drain into the canal. By the entrance one can still see the stark wooden timbers of the mine barges, which earned their name of "starvation boats" from their ribby

Something nasty lurking in the grass? Just a bollard beside the Manchester Ship Canal at Barton, Manchester.

A narrow boat crossing Barton aqueduct, which carries the Bridgewater Canal over the Manchester Ship Canal; a picture from the beginning of the century.

appearance. Once Worsley was connected to Manchester the Duke pushed on through Stretford and then to Runcorn, where the difficult descent to the River Mersey was accomplished by a flight of ten locks.

The Bridgewater cuts through some magnificent Cheshire country-side and passes pretty villages, including Lymm and Daresbury. At Lymm in outcrops of sandstone have been found the footprints of dinosaurs, many of which have been quarried and are on display in Manchester Museum. At Daresbury the canal passes atomic research laboratories and the magnificent church where Charles Dodgson's father, who was such a friend of the boat people, was vicar. The Rev Charles Dodgson, christened at All Saints Church in 1832, is better known to us as Lewis Carroll. A stained glass window in the church shows characters from *Alice in Wonderland*, and the beauty of the village remains just as Lewis Carroll records

I watch the drowsy night expire
And Fancy paints at my desire
Her Magic pictures in the fire.

An island farm, 'mid seas of corn
Swayed by the wandering breath of morn
The happy spot where I was born.

Just before the locks drop into Runcorn stands Norton Priory, which has a most fascinating history. Originally founded as an Augustinian priory in the twelfth century, Norton flourished to such an extent that it was raised to the status of an abbey. Not many Augustinian houses reached these dizzy heights but this did not save it from Henry VIII and it was dissolved in 1536. In 1545 the ruins were bought by the Brooke family, who built an imposing house on the site, this Tudor half timbered building being replaced in the eighteenth century by a Georgian mansion. This was demolished in 1928, and until 1970 the area was an overgrown wilderness. The Runcorn Development Corporation cleaned up the site, excavated the area well enough to reveal the dimensions of the old abbey as well as some sandstone tombstones, fascinating mosaic tiling and the Norman doorway, dated 1180, which is the finest in Cheshire. The Priory is now under the control of the Norton Priory Museum Trust, which is registered as a charity. Entry fees and the sale of guide books are ploughed back into further investigation and restoration. Anyone thinking that canals cut only through areas of industrial dereliction would do well to follow the winding path of the Old Duke's Canal, which to do it justice would require a volume to itself.

The Rochdale Canal connects with the Duke's canal and climbs beyond Oldham into the valley of the Roch, before rising still higher into the Pennines and ending at Sowerby Bridge in Yorkshire where it joined the Calder and Hebble Navigation which leads into the Aire and Calder. John Rennie first surveyed the route but it was 1794 before approval was obtained and by 1804 William Jessop had supervised its construction; Lancashire and Yorkshire were in direct contact by water for the first time. Its importance was fully realised and each of its thirty-three miles and a staggering ninety-two locks provided water deep enough to allow even craft from Ireland and the Isle of Man to pass through from Liverpool to the East Coast via the Mersey and Irwell Navigation and then the Rochdale.

In 1822 amid great pomp and ceremony an ornate and castellated gateway was opened at the entrance to the canal company's wharf at Dale Street, Manchester. Despite the construction of a car park on the site the splendid arch remains, along with some of the warehouses. The coffers of the company were substantially increased in 1839 when the Manchester and Salford Junction Canal was cut to link the Rochdale with the Ashton, Huddersfield, Irwell Navigation and the Manchester, Bolton and Bury canals.

As the Duke of Bridgewater had foreseen, however, the railways were rapidly overcoming their teething troubles and could operate more quickly and did not have the problem of freezing solid in winter. The

Leeds and Manchester Railway, opened in 1841, was the first beat of the death knell of the Rochdale Canal. Following a carefully planned strategy, the railway company took a lease on the canal in 1855 which guaranteed its shareholders a handsome dividend for a period of twenty-one years. Although the canal company purchased boats of its own in 1887 and continued to operate them up to 1914, when steam barges were in common use, the days of canal transport were numbered. By 1921 things were bad, and they were to get worse as road transport improved. By 1952 it had become impossible to travel from one end of the cut to the other and on 29th May, 1958, the last barge made its leisurely journey from Bloom Street power station alongside the busy streets of Manchester and out into the Bridgewater. The commercial life of the Rochdale Canal was at an end.

Fortunately the Rochdale Canal Society have been working to open the whole length of the canal to pleasure craft, and their uphill task is, at the time of writing, being blessed with some success.

The Ashton-under-Lyne Canal connected with both the Rochdale

Opposite: The Watch House on the Bridgewater Canal at Stretford dates from before the building of the canal. The lookouts who inhabited it gave warning of the Mersey flooding.

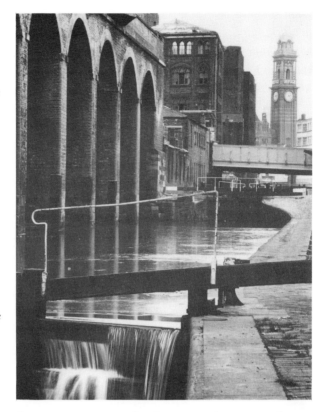

Right: Locks on the Rochdale Canal as it approaches Castlefields, in the middle of Manchester.

and the Bridgewater and serves to emphasise a point not always appreciated. The connection of river systems by artificial cuts not only allows boats to pass from one river to another but also allows plants and animals to do the same thing. With its locking systems and the movement of traffic a canal should be considered as a slow-moving river rather than a confined pond. Plants such as arrowhead and Canadian pondweed are frequently found growing in canals while meadowsweet, water mint, monkey flower, water forget-me-not and yellow flag add sweet smells and delightful variations in colour to canal and riverside. These sights are often brought by canals directly into town centres.

The Ashton canal joined the Huddersfield, which also traversed the rolling hills of the Pennines. The 5,415 yard long Standedge tunnel was built at the highest point of any canal in Britain to carry the water into the centre of Huddersfield and its ultimate connection with waterways leading to the East Coast. From the point of view of canals associated with the Mersey and its tributaries, the connection of the Ashton with the Peak Forest Canal at Dukinfield is important.

Many sections of the fourteen-and-a-half mile Peak Forest Canal with its sixteen locks have been imaginatively restored and now hum gently with leisure craft, while naturalists wander happily along the flower-rich towpaths. From the complex of locks and the aqueduct at Marple over the River Goyt the route is particularly attractive. The Peak Forest also has a smaller aqueduct to carry it across the Tame. At Whaley Bridge there is a complex of six swing bridges and at Romiley and elsewhere the Peak Forest has added to the delights of the area without detracting from the value of the rivers. Now that the clean-up operations seem to be gathering momentum, what was once one of Britain's most industrialised areas is beginning to be a popular holiday spot.

Manchester's ring of canals continued to the north, where the Manchester, Bolton and Bury played such an important part in the industrial development of the Croal-Irwell valley. The canal was unfortunately closed in 1948, but although part of the route has been drained there is sufficient part remaining for its value to be appreciated. Its days were numbered from the time it became in 1831 the first canal to amalgamate with a railway company which built its track along the same basic route. This was completed in 1838.

The route to Liverpool, fast becoming the country's second most important seaport, was increasingly popular once the Duke of Bridgewater's Canal had paved the way. Slightly to the north and west of Manchester the Worsley cut was linked to the new Leeds and Liverpool Canal via a section cut through the coalfields around Leigh. The old-established Mersey and Irwell Navigation was still busy, especially when it was linked to the Rochdale. The construction of the Macclesfield Canal provided yet another link in the chain by connecting Manchester to the Peak Forest Canal.

The city of Manchester was far from happy with the situation as it stood. Where was the hard work being done and where was industry centred? Manchester! Who could charge high prices for shipping these goods and raise prices of raw materials by imposing high docking fees? Liverpool! There was anger that the Liverpudlians held the key to the Mersey, which was not navigable to ocean going ships (especially the new steam vessels) beyond Warrington. There were also great problems in navigating the Runcorn gap. The demand for a huge ship canal was obvious rather than imaginative.

Apart from the engineering difficulties there were bound to be problems raised by the rich merchants of Liverpool, who had one driving ambition—to be even richer! They certainly had no intention of being by-passed.

Before the construction of the ship canal the river Irwell was often a fiercesome enemy, its level sometimes rising ten feet and causing great damage to factories and also to the dwellings of the poor, especially in Salford. The 120 feet wide and 28 feet deep canal absorbed the Irwell with ease and in addition swallowed the waters of the Irk, the Medlock and a smaller tributary, the Cornbrook. As we have seen, the waters of the Mersey now mingle with the ship canal from Irlam locks to Bollin Point, so even this mighty river was tamed by one of the most impressive feats of engineering ever performed in Britain. Even this now seems to have outlived its usefulness, and in less than a hundred years its commercial life is over. Threatened with closure, the Manchester Ship Canal faces a bleak prospect.

The Manchester Basin at Ashton-under-Lyne, where the Peak Forest (left), Huddersfield (foreground) and Ashton canals combine.

Barton aqueduct over the Manchester Ship Canal seen from Barton road bridge; a modern picture to compare with that on page 60.

The Mersey itself is navigable to large ships as far as Eastham, where the canal is locked into the river. The thirty-six mile cut to Manchester was begun in 1887 and completed in 1894, with connections to the Shropshire Union Canal at Ellesmere Port, the Weaver at Weston Point, and the Mersey at four separate points, at Runcorn, Warrington, Old Quay and Weston Mersey. The Runcorn and Latchford Canal can be reached via Twenty Steps Lock and the River Irwell at Irlam. The Bridgewater also links with the ship canal via Hulme Locks and Upper Reach. At one time there was a most useful link between the Bridgewater and the ship canal via Runcorn Locks, but this has not functioned since 1966, which does seem rather a pity. There is one other interesting link (in truth not quite a link) between the two most famous canals in Britain, the Barton swing aqueduct which carries the Bridgewater over the ship canal.

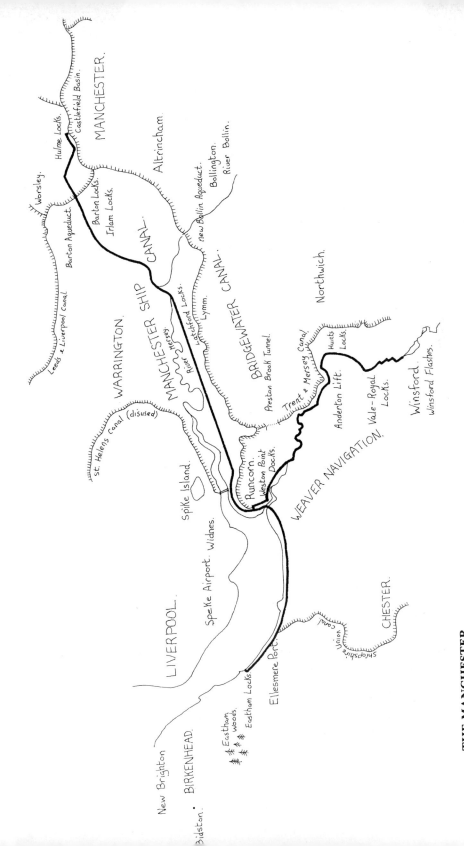

THE MANCHESTER SHIP CANAL

The digging of such a huge groove must have presented a great problem; what to do with the earth removed. Some of it was obviously used to construct embankments, but much of the spoil went into the making of Mount Manisty, looking like an ancient burial barrow between the Mersey estuary and the canal, near Eastham Locks, named after the engineer in charge of the operation. The terminus of the canal is the Manchester Docks, reached via the Mode Wheel locks. At the other side is the Pomona Docks, built on part of the site of Pomona Gardens, once Manchester's "holiday complex" fed by pleasure craft on the Irwell. There is still a link to the Irwell at this point, and also connections to the canals, including the Bridgewater, Manchester, Bury and Bolton and the Manchester and Salford Junction Canal.

During their heyday the docks throbbed to the vibrating cogs of industry, and steam and smoke belched into the air as Trafford Park evolved from a country garden into one of the world's centres of heavy industry. The ship canal directed massive tankers and cargo vessels into the heart of the city and easily coped with the railway threat which destroyed all the smaller cuts. Its turn has now come, however, for the ship canal has gradually been strangled by a noose of motorways and starved by the industrial climate of the 1970s and 1980s. Many of the heavy industries are no longer required, factories are being built in "cleaner areas", and Britain is no longer the force she was in world trade. We must accept that the ship canal as a huge profitmaking enterprise is finished.

What we must never accept is that it should fall into dereliction. What would happen to the floodwaters of the Irwell, the Medlock, the Irk and the Mersey itself? What would happen if the canal itself burst its

Snow throws the paving into sharp relief in this view of Slattocks Locks on the Rochdale Canal at Middleton, Manchester.

banks? The ship canal has an obvious amenity value. Its banks are ablaze with summer colour. Interesting alien plants accidentally brought from faraway places in cargoes mix with native species. The giant seed heads of goatsbeard are eagerly eaten by charms of goldfinches, fieldfares and redwings feed on the red haws of dog rose and the black fruits of the Burnet rose, usually confined to coastal dunes but here growing on the ash which once supported a rail track leading to a loading shed. Little grebe dive into the water, and we must not be surprised these days when they come up with a healthy looking fish. Carpets of bright yellow stonecrop and ragwort grow in profusion, contrasting with purple banks of thyme which all serve to attract a host of butterflies including the small tortoiseshell and meadow browns and day-flying moths such as the six-spot burnet and the cinnabar. There are plenty of mammals too, including hares, rabbits, short-tailed field voles and long-tailed field mice, and these attract predators such as the weasel, stoat and red fox. In recent times the North American mink has been a frequent, but far from welcome, resident.

This rich tapestry of wildlife, plus our increasing leisure time, added to the fact that a neglected ship canal would be dangerous, points the way forward. Could Pomona Docks revert to pleasure gardens? Could parks be safely left to become nature reserves? Could water sports be encouraged in other areas? Could the engineering wonders be kept running as working museums? I am sure the public would not object to paying entry fees if they knew they were helping to preserve such a magnificent old industrial route, maintaining a habitat for ourselves and wildlife and above all keeping towns along the banks of the Mersey and some of its tributaries safe from flooding.

It would be impossible to write an account, however superficial, of the canals associated with the Mersey without making reference to the industrially important Trent and Mersey and Shropshire Union canals, the historically important Sankey Brook and the sometimes confusing Compstall Navigation.

The ninety-three-mile Trent and Mersey Canal, planned by James Brindley in 1766, was not completed until 1777, by which time he was dead. The project was completed by Hugh Henshall, his brother-in-law. Initially Brindley called it the Grand Trunk Canal because it was the first to cross a major watershed, and in his eyes all other cuts were merely branches of this master navigation. To the Duke of Bridgewater, however, it was another money-spinner, and he readily agreed to link his Runcorn section to the new canal, thus giving him control over all traffic entering or leaving the tidal estuary of the Mersey. The Trent and Mersey Company spearheaded by Wedgwood was also pleased with the deal since it saved them the expense of a long navigation to the river. Wedgwood's delicate pottery was soon journeying smoothly along water instead of banging about dangerously on the back of a packhorse. The actual junction was at the northern end of Preston Brook Tunnel, but an extension to this meant that the junction is now the only one in Britain inside a tunnel, just one of the many wonders on this impressive cut. Another is a complex of thirty-five locks raising the water to a height of 408 feet just beyond Middlewich which was given the name "Heartbreak Hill", no doubt with considerable feeling. Eventually in the Harecastle region the heartbreak of an even higher climb was too much to bear and the canal builders punched a 2,880 yard tunnel through solid rock.

The Shropshire Union was another ambitious cut sixty-six-and-a-half miles long and with forty-six locks designed to bring the developing industries of the midlands, this time Wolverhampton, within reach of the port of Liverpool. Chester was another possibility, but the River Dee was already silting up rapidly and so the deep waters of the Mersey with its huge tonnage of merchant shipping were the obvious choice. There are branches to Nantwich and Middlewich, so there was some element of competition between this canal and the Weaver Navigation. It was completed in three sections opening in 1774, 1796 and 1835. At one time connecting directly with the Mersey but later linking with the Manchester Ship Canal, the Shropshire Union has its terminus at Ellesmere Port.

Sometimes referred to as the St Helens Canal and now disused, the Sankey Navigation was cut out of the Mersey at Widnes and led to Sankey Bridge near Warrington. Although opened in 1760 with a new entry opened at Fiddlers Ferry in 1764 and another at Widnes itself in 1830, it never became part of the canal system, but it can be considered as an early attempt at canal building and England's first real effort. It was originally built to connect the St Helens coalfield with the Mersey via Fiddlers Ferry.

The Compstall Navigation is unusual in the fact that it was not built to link two separated waters but was constructed in 1839 by the Andrews family, who dammed the River Etherow to provide water to drive what was then the largest water wheel in the country, built by Fairbairn Lilley and affectionately known as the "Lily Wheel". When coal was found outcropping further up the valley tub boats were soon plying back and forth supplying the mill, which now forms part of the Etherow Country Park (see Chapter One).

Before continuing the story of the Mersey we must say something about the River Bollin, which enters the ship canal at Bollin Point precisely opposite where the Mersey parts company. It was here that the old Mersey absorbed the Bollin.

CHAPTER FIVE

The Bollin and the Dean

O N THE ROLLING windswept and soggy uplands between Lancashire, Cheshire and Derbyshire rise two streams, the Bollin and the Dean, which eventually join between Wilmslow and Styal. Once merged, it is the Dean which loses its identity and the Bollin which flows on to its own union with the Manchester Ship Canal and the Mersey.

The Bollin rises in Macclesfield Forest, which, although containing belts of trees, is not a true forest and never was, being merely a well-treed hunting area. The present "forest" was planted in 1930 and consists mainly of conifers, including Corsican pine, Norway and sitka spruce and Japanese larch, although an effort has been made to include hardwood trees such as sycamore and beech.

Macclesfield Forest village stands atop a steep slope and affords views into the rolling hills of the Peak District and also to Shining Tor, one of the highest points in Cheshire and the source of the Dean. Close to the village is the source of the Goyt and the *Cat and Fiddle Inn*. This hostelry is at 1,600 feet and offers on a clear day the most magnificent views into Derbyshire and into Wales. Sheep converge on the car park and beg sandwiches and fruit from those who walk the moors. I was once having a quiet snooze in my car following a long walk over the spongy moorland when I was disturbed by a sheep banging its head on the side of the car, telling me that it was lunch time. The creature ate a hard boiled egg, a carrot, a piece of cheese and an apple pie. I had little, apart from an amusing half hour!

The weather, however, is not always so kind and a deep swirling mist often blankets the area. Highwaymen once lurked here, with easy escape routes in all directions. The modest little church in Macclesfield Forest was founded in 1673 but was rebuilt in 1834, its two most significant features being the small tower and the unusual stone altar fashioned in the form of a chalice. Rush bearing was a feature of the church, a remnant of the days when the floors were made of earth, not stone, and the ground was strewn with plants, mainly rushes but also the fragrant meadowsweet. In these highland spots rushes were also collected and peeled to expose their waxy centres, which burned dimly but without smoke. Holders for burning rush lights can still occasionally be picked up in local market stalls or second-hand shops.

The numerous Bollin brooks scattered throughout the forest are

71

gathered together to feed a complex of four reservoirs originally constructed by Macclesfield Corporation but now administered by the North West Water Authority. Two of these waters, Trentabank and Ridgegate, provide domestic and industrial water supplies while the other two, Bottoms and Teggsnose, provide compensation water for the River Bollin. In the old days a good flow was essential to drive mill machinery, and while the river no longer provides power some force is still needed to flush treated sewage out towards the Mersey and the sea. There is no direct access to Trentabank but it is clearly visible from the 20 hectare (50 acre) country park administered jointly by the water authority and the Cheshire Conservation Trust. In winter there is a rich variety of wildfowl including tufted duck, pochard and goldeneye, but its real interest is in the heronry.

In the old days the word forest simply meant an area set aside for hunting and for breeding game, which required tree cover but also open spaces to run. The locals were therefore prevented from cutting down trees or lopping off large branches. Their firewood was collected as twigs or when a tree was blown down. As the settlement of Higher Sutton is reached the infant Bollin has grown a little and we find ourselves in an area once rigidly governed by forest law. It was once called Sutton-Downes, from two families who held their lands by what was known as "the service of free forestry" and in turn were duty bound to fight for their monarch when summoned. They had a right to beasts of the forest and fish from the streams so long as the king was not in the area, and they also had the right to cut timber.

Although Sutton has some modern housing it also has its village green and some splendid buildings, including the modern church of St James, built in 1840 and enlarged and reconsecrated in 1871. The spire is particularly fine and the 1841 schoolroom below boasts one very famous pupil, the wildlife painter Charles Tunnicliffe, who completed his education at Macclesfield School of Art. The Macclesfield Canal weaves its way close to Sutton Hall, but the connection between Sutton and canals is even closer. Close to the Sutton aqueduct is a small house which was the home of Abraham Bennet, and for a while of his apprentice, James Brindley. The illiterate lad was eventually appointed chief engineer to the Duke of Bridgewater, and it was Brindley who designed the Duke's Canal.

Sutton Hall stands at the junction of two feeder streams of the Bollin and dates mainly from the seventeenth century, although one wing containing the main hall of the house is obviously much older. The hall is now looked after by caretakers after being used by the Sisters of the Poor, a group of Irish nuns. In the grounds of the hall is Sutton chapel, built in

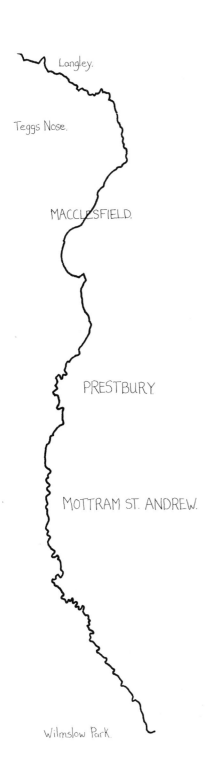

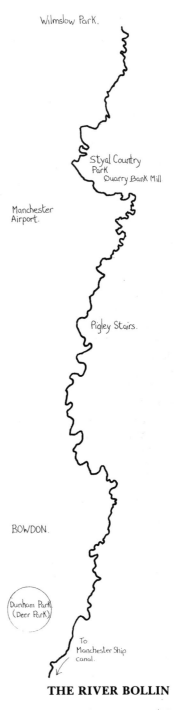

Langley.

Teggs Nose.

MACCLESFIELD.

PRESTBURY.

MOTTRAM ST. ANDREW.

Wilmslow Park.

Wilmslow Park.

Styal Country Park
Quarry Bank Mill

Manchester Airport.

Pigley Stairs.

BOWDON.

Dunham Park.
(Deer Park)

To
Manchester Ship
Canal.

THE RIVER BOLLIN

73

the sixteenth century, which in a time of religious intolerance was a sanctuary for catholics from the Macclesfield area.

To the south-east of the village is Ridge Hall Farm, on the site of an Elizabethan manor built in 1580 and the ancient seat of the Leghs. Traces of the old moat can still be detected. Three ancient pillars which used to stand in the farmyard may well be Saxon stones; they are now in West Park, Macclesfield. One interesting ex-resident of the area was John May, who lived at Ridge Hill just below the farm and played a great part in the

A curlew incubates her eggs high on the moors. *Michael Edwards*

development of Blackpool as a workers' holiday complex. He died in 1900.

Well signed both from Macclesfield and from the roads close to the Bollin is Tegg's Nose, a 54 hectare country park set up by Cheshire County Council. Tegg's Nose means Sheep's Nose, and it was named from the shape of its craggy cliffs. A famous pink stone was quarried here from the fifteenth century onwards. Enjoy a quiet lunch at one of the picnic tables and listen to curlew and soaring lark. Wander through the bracken, bilberry and gorse and look for the ring ouzel in summer and twite and red grouse all the year round. The views from this outcrop of Pennine gritstone is truly magnificent; it is at its best in the cool of a

74

winter's morning just after rain, when the streams flood into the Bollin which rushes on towards Macclesfield.

A strangely attractive confusion of a town, Macclesfield boasts buildings both ancient and modern, some set around level squares, others lining steep-sided streets. Some areas are smooth, others cobbled; market traders dovetail their stalls among the permanent shops. On the Tuesday, Friday and Saturday markets the town is a bustle of activity. Dominated by the historic church of St Michael set high on a hill, Macclesfield has not treated its river very well, and the narrow course of the Bollin has been culverted under road and rail as the town expanded to become the focal point of Britain's silk industry. There is plenty of speculation but not a lot of fact to show that Macclesfield was once a fortified town complete with defensive wall breached by three gates known as Chester, Jordan and Wall gate, all now long gone but still retained in street names. St Michael's almost resembles a castle, its dark-towered bulk being set on a pinnacle of rock and reached by no fewer than 108 well-worn cobbled steps. For those weak in wind and limb there are many good car parks at the top of the town within easy strolling distance of the church, flanked by the police station on one hand and quaint old buildings on the other.

Close by is the information centre, and the library, although some distance away, is worth a visit for those interested in the history of the silk industry. From the seventeenth century Macclesfield had a well organised cottage industry producing buttons fashioned from copper and covered with silk. By the dawn of the eighteenth century water power was being harnessed to drive thread manufacturing machinery, and Charles Roe opened Macclesfield's first silk mill in 1743. Indeed silk thread preceded cotton. Bridge Street was built during the early spread of the old town to cope with the increased population flowing in to work in silk. A new grammar school was built and in 1775 Charles Roe financed the building of the New Church out of his profits from silk, its construction taking the staggeringly short time of seven months! It was renamed Christ Church and heard its first sermon on Christmas Day, 1775; there can have been few more controversial utterances from its pulpit since. The Reverend David Simpson said

> Mr Roe has built you a house of several thousand pounds expense. Was it done to serve me after I was excluded from the other church? No, I had opportunities to go elsewhere. Was it done out of resentment to satisfy a party spirit? No, this could not be, for he had intended to build several years before the quarrel arose. What then was his reason? His motive, I verily believe, Oh Christians, was to advance the glory of God, the furtherance of the Gospel, the reformation of his fellow creatures and the salvation of souls.

The rumblings of a major ecclesiastical row can be heard in these words. It seems that Charles Roe and David Simpson had met in Buckinghamshire and had become friends. As Roe's business in Macclesfield flourished he may well have used his influence to install his friend as vicar of St Michael's, but Simpson's leaning towards Methodism annoyed some of the congregation who petitioned the Bishop of Chester, who bowed to this pressure and removed the vicar. The sermon is now clearly seen as the response to mischievous tongues spreading the rumour that Roe had built his friend another church out of spite rather than religious zeal. There may even have been the fear that Simpson's firebrand preaching would attract a following, with a corresponding reduction in the coffers of St Michael's and All Angels'. Both the old and the new church now live together in peace and harmony, St Michael's being one of the most impressive in Cheshire.

Founded by Queen Eleanor of Castile, wife of Edward I, in 1278, St Michael's was obviously built on the site of an earlier church and there is a fine collection of Saxon stones near the altar. The name Macclesfield may well be Saxon in origin, deriving from a personal name, Macca. In the Domesday Book it is called Maxfield and described as a "wasted manor" but the banks of the Bollin are known to have been settled long before the birth of Christ. It seems that Queen Eleanor loved the area and her church remains, as do its two magnificent side chapels.

The Legh chapel was built in 1422 to house the body of the Agincourt veteran Sir Piers Legh. The family were faithful servants of kings and Perkin Legh followed both Edward III and his son, the Black Prince, in their French campaigns and fought so hard and well at the battle of Crecy that Lyme park was given to him. Perkin also proved a bonny fighter for Richard II, but on this occasion the family backed the wrong horse and he was captured with Richard and was beheaded at Chester on the orders of Henry IV. Among the splendid brasses in the chapel is a memorial to Perkin which reads

> Here lyeth the body of Perkin a Legh
> That for King Richard the death did die;
> Betray'd for righteousness;
> And the bones of Sir Peere his sone
> That with King Henrie the fifth did wonne
> in Paris

The second Sir Piers was killed at Agincourt, and in memory of the two faithful warriors Sir Peter Legh built the chapel, which was dedicated in 1626. The Savage Chapel was founded in 1504 by Thomas Savage and his wife Katherine, sister of the first Earl of Derby. Thomas and Sir John Pereyvale apparently planned the chapel, together with the provision of a Chantry priest who was to perform the double function of celebrating a daily service and teaching in the nearby grammar school. The chantry had chambers above it to serve as living and sleeping accommodation for the priest.

The Savage Chapel is famous for its brasses, one showing Roger Legh kneeling with his six sons—he also had a wife and six daughters, but these are not figured—and above them is a portrayal of Pope Gregory in prayer asking Christ to fill the communion table. There are many alabaster figures depicting the Legh family, some with their favourite dogs at their feet.

Macclesfield's connections with war continued over the centuries and in 1487 after the Battle of Bosworth the aldermen petitioned the new king, Henry VII, and the first of the Tudor line, to reduce the number of troops they were obliged to supply, because of the casualties sustained in the historic battle. During the Civil War of the 1640's Macclesfield was taken by the parliamentarian Sir William Brereton following a siege. Sir

Looking down 108 Steps at Macclesfield which provide an approach to the historic St Michael's Church.

William held on to the town in the face of a bombardment from cannons directed by Sir Thomas Acton, in the course of which the spire of St Michael's was slightly damaged. The peace of the town was again shattered in 1745 when the Young Pretender, Bonnie Prince Charlie, passed through with his army of around 5,000 Scots on the way to his historic debacle at Derby. One can imagine the tired horses drinking their fill in the cool crystal waters of the Bollin, the Scots looking up at the "fortified" church on the hill and being reminded of their own Edinburgh castle perched on its rock many a long mile to the north.

As it leaves Macclesfield the Bollin swings to the north-west and flows through open country lined with alder, willow and ash, becoming noticeably cleaner as it nears the charmingly historic village of Prestbury, arguably the most fascinating in the whole of the Mersey watershed.

The name Prestbury literally means "Priest's Town", the settlement

Macclesfield Church, set high on its hill.

being known in Saxon times as Preostburgh. There seems no doubt that a substantial pre-Norman settlement existed here and this was substantiated by the discovery in 1841 of part of an eighth century sandstone cross which had been built into the wall of the church. Although Butley Hall is mentioned in the Domesday Book, why is there no mention of Prestbury? We sometimes forget that the rule of the Normans was not accepted willingly and both sides fought hard and long, the Saxons and their foes both adopting a scorched earth policy.

The eighth century cross is now in the churchyard and protected under glass, a brass tablet bearing the following inscription:

> These fragments of ancient Art forming part of a cross, erected by our Saxon forefathers a thousand years ago, to commemorate, as is believed the first preaching of Christianity in this place, were found embedded in the walls of the church, where in a mutilated state they had remained concealed from view for full four centuries in the hope that they will be preserved for future generations as a treasured landmark of our past history.

It is likely that the first Christian building would have been erected nearby and the waters of the Bollin near the present bridge would have served admirably for the baptism of converts.

In the churchyard stands an impressive structure known as "The Norman Chapel", with a magnificent twelfth century arch and, over the door, a tympanum depicting Christ in Majesty. The church guide book describes the seven unique figures, now much eroded, which are above the tympanum:

> The central figure represents God the Father holding the law in His left hand typified by an open book, and the Gospel in the right hand as foreshadowed by the cross; conjointly justice and mercy are portrayed. The figure to the right with the animal (the Norman method of drawing a lamb) seems to stand for Christ, the lamb of God seated at the right hand of the Father. The figure to the left, having a resemblance to a bird, typifies the Holy Ghost in the form of a dove. Collectively these figures stand for the Trinity. St Peter with the Key is shown in the sixth figure. To this Saint the Church was dedicated as is its successor at the present day. Figure two represents the monarch who reigned when the oratory was built and this was almost certainly Richard I, Coeur de Lion, he being the first of the Norman kings to bear the budded sceptre surmounted by the plain cross as here shown. This brings the date of the oratory within the year of his coronation, 1190, and that of his death 1199. The warrior with battle axe and priest with staff represent the military and ecclesiastical government of the county palatine. These figures may be, when taken together, interpreted as follows "In the name of the Blessed Trinity, this church dedicated to St Peter was built by the abbot and monks of St Werburgh in the reign of Richard I when Randle Blunderville was Earl of Chester".

Once replaced by the present church around 1220, the old chapel gradually decayed and would probably have disappeared altogether if it had not been taken over and restored by Sir William Meredith, the

Mayor of Macclesfield in 1762, to be used as a family tomb. In 1977 new windows were designed by Francis Skeat in memory of Ann Hogarth Rogers, the popular wife of the vicar. The six windows are based on a poem discovered carved on an old grandfather clock in Chester Cathedral:

> When as a child I laughed and wept, time crept
> When as a youth I dreamed and talked, time walked
> When I became a full grown man, time ran
> And later as I grew older time flew
> Soon I shall find while travelling on, time gone
> Will Christ have saved my soul by then? Amen

It seems strange to talk about the "modern" church when it was built in 1220 and especially when it is so full of history. The impressive tower overlooks the main street on which stands the well preserved fourteenth century half timbered "priest house", now the local branch of the National Westminster Bank. Close by are the old stocks.

The original nave and choir of the 1220 period remain, but the south aisle was built around 1310 and the square tower and porch date from 1480. A gravestone preserved in the chancel is inscribed in the name of Reginald Legh, dated 1482 and gives him credit for having been a "helper" during the construction of the tower. The churchwardens' accounts make fascinating reading and throw some light on the natural history of the area over the centuries. In 1731 a public meeting was held in the vestry to discuss the problem caused by animal pests. A reward of 6d. (2½p) for every mole was offered and the head of an otter brought the substantial reward of 7s. 6d. (37½p). An engraving in the church shows a fisherman on the Bollin; he would doubtless have looked at the otter's success in catching trout with envy and wished to exterminate his

rival. Things have not changed! The engraving is dated 1819; the pollution from Macclesfield's silk works would soon remove both the fish and the otters which fed upon them. The river is now cleaner than in the heyday of silk, and trout once more glide among the stones in the soft bed of the Bollin, but will the otter ever return?

Prestbury village itself is built, ribbon-like, on each side of the main street, which in addition to the "Priests-House-Bank" has some splendid old inns including the *Black Boy* which dates to 1403 and in former years was once confusingly called *The Legh Arms*. Pearl Street runs from the main road towards the old ford used before the Bollin was bridged. The name sets me wondering about the possibility of an ancient pearl fishery close by, since the freshwater mussel *Anodonta* occasionally contains a growth which we more usually associate with oysters. The Romans certainly exploited British rivers for pearls, and perhaps the Bollin was one of them. Or is there another explanation? When the river was bridged in the sixteenth century the main road was diverted via New Street. The present bridge was built in 1885.

The old and new churches at Prestbury. On the opposite page is the Norman chapel which was replaced by the present church in the thirteenth century, and on the right the "new" church, with the stocks in the foreground.

The village is sandwiched between two splendid halls which may be likened to a couple of bookends supporting a row of truly historic "volumes" including corn mills, cottages, quaint shops, a school and, of course, the church and inns. At the south end of the village is the white painted Prestbury Hall, built in the early fifteenth century and the birthplace of Sir Richard Sutton, who founded Brazenose College at Oxford. There have been considerable alterations and renovations, but the present owners have retained much of the glory of the grand old building.

Butley Hall to the north of the village is even older, and merits a mention in Domesday where it was listed as the property of Ulric, a Saxon freeman who must have been a good friend of the Normans to have been allowed to retain his lands. Eventually the estate came into the possession of the Piggot family, who donated some of the estate to the monks of St Werburg's Abbey. By 1574 the Davenports were in residence, and the Leghs of Adlington purchased the land in 1735. Since this date the hall has been home to several of Prestbury's vicars and it was refaced during the eighteenth century. The area around the hall has, however, been settled since before written records were made. This was clearly shown in 1808 when a series of cairns was discovered on the northern side of the hall. Human bones and pottery, possibly of neolithic origin, were removed. The whole of the Bollin valley was almost certainly settled during this period and by Saxon times a ribbon of villages had developed along it, including Mottram St Andrew.

This snug village with its Saxon cross was originally known as Mottram Andrew, the Saint being introduced by the Victorians in an effort to keep up with the pretentions of the age. The tiny village has retained all its charm and seems to have been forgotten by time. At one time there were copper mines here, and during the early part of the nineteenth century Sir Henry Roscoe, a professor at Manchester University, spent some time investigating the old mines. It was here that he discovered the ore from which he extracted a new element, which we know as Vanadium. It is a metal which melts at 1720°C and is used in the manufacture of high speed steels; it also alloys well with chromium.

Around the village are some fascinating buildings but none of them is open to the public. Legh Hall is first recorded in 1388 and Spittal House was once the site of a leper hospital complex under the protection of St Werburg's Abbey. Nothing remains of the original buildings apart from one cruck barn. Very few of these now remain in England but the north-west and Cheshire in particular has a goodly supply of these Saxon-designed barns. The idea was simple, the whole structure being supported by huge boughs of oak, the weight of the building being borne by the natural grain of the timber. The Spittal House barn dates from around 1350.

From its winding course close to the tiny unspoiled Mottram the Bollin runs onwards to Wilmslow, also a one-time Saxon village but now a dormitory for the mighty Manchester. Standing proud on a bluff of sandstone once called Williams Hill, St Bartholomew's Church overlooks the River Bollin. There was certainly a religious house here in 1264 but it is likely that a Saxon church or perhaps a lookout post was sited at the spot. Wilmslow derives its name from this hill.

The present church owes its attraction to the influence, and probably also to the money, of Henry Trafford, its rector during the period of its enlargement from 1516-1537. Some of the church, a spiral staircase near the altar for example, is obviously thirteenth century in origin. Decay had set in by the mid-nineteenth century and a major restoration was needed, but what was done seems to have amounted to legalised vandalism; altar tombs, oak pews and decorative and irreplaceable screens were removed without apparent thought. Some splendid sixteenth century screens only survived because work planned around 1898 could not be completed because the necessary funds were lacking. Some impressive artefacts do remain, however, including the tombs of the Newton family and of Henry Trafford himself, the Hawthorne chapel and a brass to commemorate Sir Robert Booth, the oldest in Cheshire. This has been dated

The old Priest House at Prestbury, now in use as a bank.

at 1460 and is contained in the Prescott chapel. The inscription is somewhat worn but reads

> Here lies the body of Robert del Bouthe, Knight, formerly Lord of Bolyn, Thorneton and Durham, who died on the feast of Saint Edith the Virgin [September 16th] in the year of our Lord 1460. And the body of Douce wife of the said Robert del Bouthe who died on the morrow of the feast of Saint Tecla the virgin in the year of our Lord 1453.
>
> To whose souls may God favour. Amen.

The name Bolyn is of interest here, for it is often said that Anne Boleyn, second wife of Henry VIII and mother of Queen Elizabeth, was a Cheshire lass, but evidence that she had lived in a long-demolished manor house on the banks of the Bollin at Wilmslow is impossible to substantiate. What is equally interesting and not in dispute is that Sir William Brereton of nearby Alderley became Groom to the Queen's Bedchamber and was beheaded on Henry's orders for alleged misconduct with Anne Boleyn. The brass in Wilmslow Church does at least show that Bolyns (or Boleyns) were present in the area and that the future Queen could have worshipped here. Her eyes may well have rested on pieces of stained glass which experts have dated at 1523. It is much more certain that as a youth William Ewart Gladstone worshipped here, long before he became one of the greatest of Victorian Prime Ministers.

There are few finer ways to spend a summer's evening than sitting in the landscaped garden of remembrance below the church and listening to St Bartholomew's peal of seven bells mingling with the gentle rippling of the Bollin, which runs close by. Over the years the river has been raised, lowered, speeded up, dammed and occasionally culverted to serve the needs of Wilmslow or to protect its houses from flood. The town is, however, not without its open spaces and it was here that Bramwell Evans, better known as "Romany" of the BBC and the first to bring natural history to the forefront on radio, spent the latter part of his life. At Parkway his distinctive green and white gypsy caravan is preserved as a memorial to him.

Samuel Finney, Queen Caroline's favourite portrait painter, was also a Wilmslow lad. He wrote *A Historical survey of the Parish of Wilmslow*, which for a piece of eighteenth century writing reads surprisingly like a modern guide book. As his fame grew Finney was appointed a magistrate; he did much to bring the rowdy elements in the town to heel. Doubtless his firmness was approved by the Quakers, who had established a meeting house in the town despite persecution meted out to them in the seventeenth century.

Close to the river and beyond the church is an area known as the Carrs, criss-crossed with footpaths and surprisingly attractive despite its industrial past. Once damp and fertile common land, then drained and partly industrialised, the area was given by Henry Buddington of Pownall Hall to the people of Macclesfield in 1925 to be used as a park. Here was the eighteenth century Carrs silk mill, conveniently sited on the Bollin banks. Although the mill was burned down in 1923 traces of its walls can still be seen, as can the weir and the mill pond. The construction of the mill did involve some alteration to the course of the river, and in recent years other "modifications" have been deemed necessary. In 1968, for example, the meander of the Bollin was "corrected" to prevent erosion both of a miniature golf course in the park and of the bridge. In 1972 part of the river bank was strengthened with concrete to prevent flooding. It was not only Wilmslow itself which caused alterations to the river running through the town, but demands were also made by the Gregs of Styal mill further downstream.

Quarry Bank Mill at Styal on the Bollin, now preserved by the National Trust and open to the public as a museum.

The delightful old village of Styal with its half timbered black and white inns, quaint cottages with gardens full of roses and hollyhocks and scented by sweet peas has not been spoiled by the building of some modern houses with red roofs nor by the presence of a prison for women.

It is reached via well-signed routes to Styal Country Park, set around Samuel Greg's Quarry Bank Mill, built in 1784. This continued to produce cotton until 1959 and is now run by the National Trust as a museum. The mill was powered originally by the Bollin, whose waters had just been supplemented by those of the Dean, the two joining at the aptly named Twinnies Bridge. The name derives from the old word "Twistle", which means a confluence. A bridge was built of iron in 1878 and there had been, judging by the local field names, a mill on this site in the past. Historians have been able to date one such building to 1335 and "higher and lower mill fields" are still marked on maps today. These, however, would have been corn mills and not the mighty industrial complexes of downstream Styal.

Now liberally provided with car parks, visitors' centre and well-planned walks through the wooded valley, Styal Country Park offers a day to remember for all the family. Paths suitable for wheelchairs run from the car park at Twinnies Bridge into Willow Ground Wood, rich in flower fragrance and bird song, and from the main car park down into the mill complex. Styal lies in the middle reaches of the Bollin and figures prominently in the Bollin Valley Project, a well-wardened scheme financed mainly by the Cheshire County Council.

Samuel Greg was much more than a cotton manufacturer. When he opened his mill Styal was a mere hamlet and accommodation had to be provided for his workers, so in 1790 he built the apprentice house which accommodated up to a hundred children from the local workhouse. I have heard the cynical suggest that he should not have been allowed to exploit the young in this manner, yet there are two sides to the coin. A display showing conditions within the apprentice house makes it clear that these were much better than anything the poor mites could have expected in the outside world, and they must have had some cause to love Samuel Greg. In 1797 he built Quarry Bank House, privately owned still, as are many of Styal's cottages—a fact which visitors should consider as they stroll around the village searching for facts and photographs. Styal is developing all the time, and it is hoped that the plan to set up a museum of the cotton industry comes to fruition.

It really is a case of ancient and modern in this area, for Manchester's Ringway airport with its system of link roads and runways lies very close to the river. The next large settlement washed by Bollin water is Bowden, but between it and Styal are some interesting spots, including Pigley Stairs and Ross Mill. Pigley Stairs consists of fields alongside the river bank which make ideal picnic spots. I once sat here early on a July morning and watched a dog fox swim the Bollin; after shaking himself dry he rolled happily in the grass before trotting off to his daytime hideout. Ross Mill is another riverside picnic spot fringed by beech trees, a delight for chaffinches, which are joined in winter by bramblings, a migrant finch from northern Europe and Scandinavia. The marshland abounds with dragonflies and is a glorious flush of summer colour as ragged robin, yellow iris, water mint and forget-me-not burst into bloom. Whitethroats sing from the scrubland, and the well-planned pony trail ensures that the snort of trotting horses adds the final touch of old England.

A red fox, often seen by the Bollin.

Bowden is another of the Bollin's Saxon villages expanded by the demands of the Manchester conurbation and its closeness to an international airport. Bowden has, however, retained its Saxon links in its name (Bode = home Don = a plain on a rising hill). The church site is on this hill, and the adjacent village square and its old cottages leading down Church Brow have changed little over the centuries. St Mary's Church has a splendid ninety-foot tower and pinnacles, plus a magnificent pulpit and windows. The interior is characterised by some lovely woodwork, sensibly retained when the old church almost fell apart and was restored in 1858. The new church, built of sandstone, retains many old features and artefacts. There is a fourteenth century monument depicting Sir William Baguley, and another showing William and Jane Brereton of Ashley, plus their seven children kneeling beneath them. Another prominent family depicted in marble by the sculptor Andre Carpentiere is the Booths of Dunham. This remarkable family played an important role in the seventeenth and eighteenth century history of England in general and their own area in particular. The Booths were raised to the peerage, taking the name of Delamere, and were further elevated when they became Earls of Warrington.

The first substantial building at Dunham Massey was a castle constructed by Hamo de Masci, who rebelled against Henry II. Still standing in 1323, the castle was moated and must have been important in its time. An Elizabethan-style hall was built around 1616, but this was largely remodelled in the 1730s by John Norris on the orders of the Earl of Warrington. The family have looked after their lovely home well and it is now open to the public and administered by the National Trust. The gardens and deer park are impressive both scenically and historically.

In the days when fresh meat was difficult to guarantee, deer parks served more as a larder than for sport. Originally native red deer would be the species confined, but fallow were popular introductions during the eighteenth and nineteenth centuries, their huge palmated antlers being very decorative indeed. They are also more even-tempered during the rut than the stamping, snorting, stinking red deer. In 1844 there were about five hundred fallow deer, but at the present time the herd numbers about three hundred head. Another typical mammal of this beech-dominant park is the grey squirrel, deliberately introduced from North America between 1870 and 1930 to add beauty to the British fauna. So successful has it become that it has now been labelled as ugly, which it clearly is not, and as a destructive pest, which it equally clearly is. Those fascinated by old country crafts would do well to park on Charcoal Road, near the lodge house, and stroll to the remains of a charcoal pit; charcoal burning was once an important industry in these woodlands.

On the river just out of Dunham Park is the five-storeyed Bollington corn mill, the banks of the Bollin being raised to provide a greater head of water. The waterwheel was of the undershot design, meaning that the current of water strikes the floats of the wheel at the bottom and drives it round, in contrast to the overshot wheel, where the water drops on to the wheel at the top, its sheer weight turning the wheel. Little is left of the original machinery; the mill is now used as a garden fertiliser store after a period of use as a refrigerated cheese store.

On goes the Bollin under the Bridgewater Canal and along a flat plain to Bollin Point, where it oozes gently into the Manchester Ship Canal. On the opposite bank of the canal the River Mersey leaves the cut through which it has flowed for several miles and continues its journey to Warrington. Before returning to the Mersey brief consideration must be given to the Dean and the Birkin, the Bollin's two most important tributaries.

High on Shining Tor the Dean begins its twisting course towards

Twinney Bridge. From Rainow village there are splendid views over magnificent walking country, stout stone cottages, old parish stocks, and a modern church. Robin Hood seems to have covered a lot of ground, for outside his inn at Rainow is a verse which reads:-

My ale is fine! my spirits good!
So stop and drink with Robin Hood.
If Robin Hood is not at home,
Stop and drink with Little John.

Pott Shrigley is another Deanside upland village at the junction of five tree-lined cloughs and with a lovely church surrounded by the black and white buildings so typical of Cheshire. The church has an impressive tower and peculiar grinning carvings around its walls and under the chancel arch. Most of the building was constructed in the fifteenth century, but there is an effective modern stained glass window depicting among other things a rabbit and a water-mill. Overlooking the once important cotton spinning village is the 900 foot bulk of the hill called White Nancy.

Before meeting the Bollin the Dean oozes gently between its wood-lined banks past Adlington and Handford, both of which have historic halls. The latter building has a huge beamed doorway containing the date of building, 1562, and a carving of a bear's head, the crest of the Brereton family. In the Civil War it was the base of that pugnacious supporter of Parliament William Brereton. He proved a most able military commander, capturing Beeston Castle and inflicting a severe defeat on the Royalists at Middlewich. Apparently he intended to be buried in the church at Cheadle, but his body was lost in the Mersey.

And Bollin, that along doth nimbler Birkin bring
From Maxfield's mightie wildes

So wrote Michael Drayton in *Polyolbion*, published in 1620. The gentle Birkin drains an historic area of halls and horticulture around Knutsford and Chelford. It picks up Marthall Brook and Pedley Brook at Chelford and Mobberley Brook from the historic village of the same name. Here was born George Mallory, who in 1924 perished with Andrew Irvine on the upper slopes of Mount Everest. The National Trust own some twenty acres around St Wilfrid's Church, which is justly proud of its rood screen, made around 1500. There is also some very impressive stained glass in the church. Around it snuggle lovely black and white half timbered houses, so typical of Cheshire.

The Bollin and its tributaries flow through the best of the Cheshire countryside, which is another factor supporting the statement that those who try to follow the watershed of the Mersey will observe a greater contrast with regard to scenery than anywhere else in Britain.

CHAPTER SIX

Irlam to Warrington

HARRISON the sixteenth century historian described this stretch of the Mersey thus:-

> After his confluence with Irwell the Mersey runneth to Partington, and not far from there entertaineth the Glass or Glassbrook water, increased by sundry arms, whereof one cometh from Lodward, another from above Houghton, the third from Hulton Park and the fourth from Shakerley and being all united near unto Leigh, the confluence goeth to Holcroft, and above Hollin Green into the swift Mersey.

An old poem boldly states that

Irk, Irwell, Medlock and Tame
When they do meet with Mersey
Do lose their name.

At the time both these pieces were written the Mersey flowed a great deal quicker than it does now, the flow having slowed because of improved drainage and of the construction of the ship canal. The Mersey itself loses its name from its entry into the ship canal at Irlam Weir, the two sharing a common course before separating opposite the point where the river Bollin enters; the Mersey then follows its ancient meandering route to Warrington and beyond this ancient town to the sea. One of the old meanders lost when the canal was built was Rixton Leys, which was a water meadow close to the point where the Glazebrook merged with the old Mersey. In the villages of Irlam, Warburton, Hollins Green, Thelwall and Latchford industry has never quite swamped all the old riverside tranquility.

Standing at Irlam Weir watching the Mersey crash into the ship canal, leaving a wall of detergent froth and debris trapped in a series of grids, I found myself with mixed feelings. The river is polluted, but not nearly so badly as in former years. On the opposite side of the canal the old Irlam steelworks has been demolished and nature has started to claim her own. A whitethroat sang from a tangle of brambles, elderberry blossom shone like snow against the green of the leaves and a fat man with a bucket and a gleam in his eye gathered it to make elderflower wine. Down on the bank of both canal and river butterbur grew in profusion, its huge umbrella-like leaves almost six feet in height and swamping all other vegetation except for a bank of tall alders. In the limey rubble of the old steelworks a little ringed plover incubated her eggs close to the spot where a black redstart had been seen during the

90

winter. Both these rare birds have taken less than two years to make use of man-made habitat. Naturalists should never equate lack of attractive scenery with lack of interesting natural history.

Two prominent families dominated this area, the Irlams from which the name derives and the Lathoms whose Elizabethan hall was once thought to be supported by the biggest beam in the country. Until 1951 the hall was used for lectures and meetings, but it has now unfortunately been demolished, although the gates still stand close to the modern swimming pool. It was only when the beam was examined after demolition that it was found to have a false joint; its fame was destroyed. Some idea of old Irlam can be gained from the writings of James Goodier, whose recollections take us back into the last century.

> At the turn of the century one could walk along the river bank from Fairhills Road, Lower Irlam, to the meadows near Salt Eye Corner, Peel Green. Alas! Only two short lengths of this old waterway survive, that from Fairhills road to the *Boat House Inn*, and the short length running from Boysnope Wharf, Barton Moss, into the Manchester Ship Canal. The latter was opened in 1894 by Her Majesty Queen Victoria. The Old River, or to give it its proper name, the River Irwell, ran more or less parallel with the new canal from a place called Water-Meetings, which literally meant the meeting place of the rivers Mersey and Irwell and which was situated at a place on which part of the local steelworks now stands.

The steel works have now gone and a few of the sights and sounds of Old Irlam vividly remembered by James Goodier are beginning to return, although the corncrake has now gone from most of Britain, a victim not of pollution but rather of increased agricultural efficiency.

> ... if one strayed a couple of hundred yards or so from either side of Liverpool Road in Higher Irlam during springtime or early summer, one would almost certainly hear the song of the skylark, singing high in the sky; or the calls of the peewit, the corncrake, and countless other singing birds. And perhaps in the middle of all this, as one walked leisurely along, a frightened rabbit would bolt from the hedgerow and scamper across an open field to another hideout. Or, on a walk from the Old Road to the meadows along the bank of the Old River—the Irwell—one could gather in springtime such flowers as bluebells, buttercups, mayflowers, and daisies in profusion. Nowadays, alas, neither on the Moss nor in the meadows does the lark sing high in the sky, nor the corncrake cry from the field; and the bluebells, the buttercups, and the mayflowers have long since wilted under the now polluted industrial atmosphere.
>
> In those far off days one remembers there was a stillness in the air, which brooded a contentment, perhaps only known to those who have had the good fortune to enjoy a relaxed, quiet, village life. An abiding memory of that quiet, peaceful atmosphere which I still retain is of one Christmas morning in the late years of the 1890s and the sound of music floating over the still frosty air. Then as a mere youngster, I walked holding my sister's hand, along with other members of my family, to a Christmas morning service in the parish Church; it was the sound of an old, familiar Christmas hymn being played by the local brass band at some distant farm on the Moss. That haunting, yet pleasing, music I can still hear to this day.

The history of Irlam goes back to far earlier times, for in the late nineteenth century a Bronze Age canoe was dug up close to Chat Moss and sent to Salford Museum. At one time this moss was described by Defoe as "frightful to think of and will bear neither horse nor man". In 1805 it was decided to try to drain the moss, an operation that was so successful that Stephenson was able to cross it with a rail link connecting Manchester to Liverpool, supporting the line on a bed of fascines to prevent it sinking into the soft ground.

Further down the ship canal at Cadishead a sign off the A57 to the left just beyond the *Coach and Horses Hotel* leads to Bobs Lane Ferry. Although it now crosses the canal, the ferry continues an age-old tradition of a right-of-way over the Mersey which the Manchester Ship Canal Company had to honour. The diesel-engined vessel carries around a dozen passengers all through the day; should it have mechanical trouble the ferryman has to row the reserve boat. A number of years ago there was a terrible tragedy when fuel which had been spilled on the water caught fire and incinerated a number of people. Although the ferry site is surrounded by chemical works, things are much less dangerous these days. A very pleasant day can be spent by crossing the Mersey Ship Canal and following well-signed paths from Partington to the historic village of Warburton.

The old ferry house at Cadishead seen across the isolated section of the Irwell.

Here is another village named after a famous family, the Warburtons having had a manor here at least from the fourteenth century. A splendid iron bridge spans the ship canal, and beyond this visitors are often astonished to have to pay a small toll to cross another bridge over a wide damp ditch overgrown with willow and alder and coloured in spring by large clumps of celandine and kingcup. Stop and look over the bridge, for here is the old course of the Mersey, cut off when the ship canal was built, leaving the old toll bridge high but not yet quite dry. Warburton village can be then seen in its true light—an important settlement with either a ferry or a bridge over the Mersey

It is said that wives were bought and sold under the old market cross on Townfield Lane, and also that Dick Turpin hid at Warburton during one of his escapades. Whether these tales are true or not, there is no doubting that the old stocks kept offenders in place or that the thirteenth century church is worth a visit. Yet another "Warby legend" infers that the church stands on the site of a Saxon church founded by the daughter of Alfred the Great, burner of cakes. Within the present church, with its quaint brick tower at the eastern end, are lovely beams and rafters which are said to be secured not with wooden pegs but with the antlers of deer. The pillars of the nave are made not of stone but of good old English oak, another most unusual feature. If you look closely you can see the marks of the carpenter's adze on them. There is a font dated 1603 and the pulpit, altar and altar rails were fashioned later in the seventeenth century. Some of the gravestones are thought to be 750 years old.

Care must be taken to look at the correct church, since a new one was built in 1885 by Mr R. R. Egerton-Warburton. The old church is dedicated to St Werburgh, the daughter of King Wulfhere of Mercia, so it looks as if the Alfred legend may be somewhat dubious. The name Warburton (St Werburgh's tun) derives from this lady, who is buried at Chester. The "tun" gets a mention in Domesday, and a priory was built nearby by the Premonstratensian Order of monks. A field close to the old church is still called Abbey Croft.

Warburton Hall has long since gone, but Ormerod's *History of Cheshire*, published in 1882, gives a good clue where to look for evidence of its existence.

> The hall of Warburton has long ceased to be the family residence. Its moated site lies to the east side of the church and village and the adjacent field retains the name of Warburton Park.

The hall was at one time surrounded by a deer park, and the journey from Cadishead to Warburton gives the feeling of what life must have been like for travellers along the old Mersey, a sensation which is even stronger if you return to the Lancashire side and walk round the Hollins Green and Glazebrook area.

In his *New Scientist* article dated 15th March, 1984, entitled *The Great Drain Robbery* Fred Pearce listed the twenty-eight dirtiest rivers in Britain. The Mersey itself is No. 21 and its tributaries feature prominently in the list. The Roch is third, Sankey Brook fourth, the Tame twelfth, the Dane fifteenth, Irwell sixteenth, Glazebrook next and the Manchester Ship Canal twenty-seventh.

The Glazebrook, which runs from Leigh to its junction with the Mersey at Cadishead, certainly could do with a clean-up, although ugliness like beauty is often in the eye of the beholder who sees what he or she is looking for. The name comes from *Glasa*, the Old English word for bright, and there certainly are some bright spots on the Glazebrook. One of them is Hollins Green, a village which seems to have had a variety of names including Holly Fare. The derivation could either be Holly Green or Holly Ferry, and there is evidence of a ferry across the Mersey from here at least from 1352. At this time there is a record of a murder

taking place near the Hollins ferry. Nearby Rixton was named after Eric, and was Eric's tun.

At one time a brickworks extracted clay from the area and Rixton clay pits, now flooded, are a haven for wildlife. Some heated argument took place a few years ago when it was proposed to use the area as a refuse and industrial waste tip. At the moment great crested grebes, coots, moorhens and wildfowl swim happily in the flooded pits, but many of the damp areas once rich in orchids have been allowed to become flooded. Teasel still grows well here, a sign of importance in the felt-making industry, now long gone. The rough seed heads of the plants were used to raise the nap on the felt. Recent work has shown that the cup-shaped leaves which clasp the stem hold water in which flies often drown. The decaying bodies of the insects add to the diet of the plant, enabling it to grow in areas not rich in soil-based chemicals.

Local naturalists have tried hard to set up a nature reserve at Rixton

Opposite: A mute swan and cygnet. Swans are frequent visitors to Woolston Eyes.

Right: The northern marsh orchid which grows well at Rixton clay pits.

clay pits, but "experts" say it is too close to the existing reserve at Risley Moss, which has been well written up. It seems to me as a neutral observer that the area could do with another wildlife reservoir, from which flora and fauna could expand into the areas around the Glazebrook and the ship canal as they become less polluted.

Woolston Eyes and Thelwall provide a perfect example of what can be achieved when industry and conservationists work hand in hand. The

Teal at the edge of Woolston Eyes.
M. Chesworth

Manchester Ship Canal Company allow the Eyes conservation group to manage the area and issue a limited number of permits to visitors to the reserve, situated between Rixton and Warrington. The Eyes have been created in flooded areas produced in between high banks of sludge removed by boats dredging the canal to keep its channels open. From the Eyes there are splendid views over the ship canal itself and also across the meandering course of the Mersey. On the waters wildfowl are present in good numbers at all seasons; they often include the North American ruddy duck with its lovely blue bill and rusty red back typifying the male. After escaping from collections, the species is rapidly expanding its range, being more common in Cheshire than elsewhere. Bitterns and hen harriers have been seen in the surrounding reeds and the butterfly populations are spectacular.

Beyond the Eyes is the Thelwall viaduct carrying the heavy traffic of the M6 over the ship canal. Below the viaduct on the opposite side of ship canal, Bridgewater Canal and the Mersey lies the fascinating village of Thelwall, which is so difficult to find these days that its once-important role in history is not often realised. At one time Thelwall was connected to Woolston by another Mersey ferry, but this seems to have fallen into disuse during the eighteenth century after the Woolston Cut connected it to Warrington around 1720. Woolston New Cut replaced the old cut about a hundred years later, but this has not been used for almost forty years.

The name Thelwall means a pool by a plank bridge and derives from Old English. The settlement merited an entry in the Anglo-Saxon Chronicle but not in the Domesday Book. It is usually stated that the city of Thelwall was founded in 923 by Edward the Elder, and many visitors arrive expecting to see items of great antiquity; they go away disappointed. This is a great pity because there are some delightful half-timbered cottages, although we must regret that the lovely Georgian Hall was allowed to fall into disrepair and after use as a military office during the Second World War was demolished. However the inn proudly records Edward the Elder's city.

After the Norman Conquest Thelwall was in ecclesiastical hands but by 1662 it was owned by the Pickering family, and it was they who built the eighteenth century hall. In the church a stained glass window dedicated in 1950 celebrates the life of Sir Peter Rylands, who was

Wildfowl on the Eyes at Woolston, with the Thelwall viaduct carrying the M6 in the background.

involved in the manufacture of wire for which nearby Warrington is famous. Indeed the local Rugby League team is nicknamed the "Wires". As the Mersey sweeps on from Thelwall it passes Latchford and Wilderspool, both once settlements in their own right but now swallowed by the expanding town of Warrington.

The derivation of the name Wilderspool is once more Old English, the original name roughly translating as "the pool where the wild deer drink". It is mentioned in the thirteenth century, under this name, when no doubt the deer still trotted down to the pure-running shallows of the Mersey to drink their fill. Some historians believe that the Romans had a fort here at the time they were striking out from their large settlement at Chester. Its name may well have been Veratinum, but it has not yet proved possible to establish this with certainty.

When Warrington Bridge was constructed in 1305 there was a path leading towards Manchester (Stockton Heath), though for more than three hundred years the flooding of the Mersey made this route rather unreliable. In the early seventeenth century an imaginative scheme raised the causeway on stone arches over the flood water, extending the bridge for a distance of 910 yards. The old arches are still present, buried beneath layers of modern tarmacadam. When the ship canal was in its planning stages the Mersey was diverted and the old course behind the Wilderspool causeway is now filled in. The causeway has seen its share of conflict, industry and enjoyment. In 1643 the Earl of Derby's men disputed the ground in a bloody encounter with parliamentarians, and this was the route followed by those who sweated in the ironworks and those who brewed the ale to replace this lost moisture. The area is now in Greenall Whitley land, Greenall Whitley being the brewery which offended the local council by running a competition with a first prize of a week's holiday in Warrington; the second prize was two weeks in Warrington!

Another of the old Mersey crossing points was at Latchford, a name which means a ford over the laecc, a stream. Although absorbed by Warrington as long ago as 1847, Latchford like Thelwall may well have been occupied by the forces of Edward the Elder in A.D. 923. The Latchford district now stretches from Warrington Bridge to the south of the Manchester Ship Canal, the building of which caused considerable disruption to old Latchford. It was in 1801, however, that Latchford— which had held its own fair from 1367—first felt the wind of change. In that year the Old Quay Canal was opened and boats were able to move downstream to Runcorn without having to wait for a suitable tide. When the ship canal was constructed an extensive system of locks was built at Latchford along with two high level bridges and one huge swing bridge.

This transport complex has swallowed a great deal of old Latchford but not all, as a stroll among the old cottages amply proves.

Now regarded as an industrial town, Warrington was a vital connection between Lancashire and Cheshire via Latchford from the time of the Romans, many of whose artefacts have been found locally, including a baby's feeding bottle made of clay and now kept in the municipal museum and art gallery in Bold Street. The Normans, too, knew Warrington well and crossed the Mersey by a wooden bridge. This was rebuilt in 1364 and a completely new structure appeared in 1495, amid great controversy. "The Legend of Bewsey Hall" with all its grisly details was recorded by Frank Hird in his *Lancashire Stories*, published around 1911.

In the ancient days the Butlers of Bewsey Hall were lords of the manor at Warrington. Originally the family name had been Pincerna, but an ancestor acting as butler to Ranulph, Earl of Chester in 1158, had taken the surname of Butler from his office. The position of butler to so great a nobleman as the Earl of Chester was not a menial office, but was equivalent to that of a Comptroller, or Master, of the Household, in a royal household of our own time, and could only be held by a knight of good family. In later generations the descendant of the first Butler married the heiress of Matthew Villiers, Lord of Warrington, and so became possessed of Bewsey Hall and its surrounding property.

Amongst the many rights appertaining to the lord of the manor of Warrington was that of a ferry across the Mersey, which was the only communication between the Lancashire and Cheshire sides, a monopoly which brought a goodly number of groats each year to the Butler coffers. This monopoly continued until the reign of Henry VII, and was the actual cause which led to Sir John Butler's murder. Henry VII, being about to pay his historic visit to his step-father, the first Earl of Derby, at Latham House, it was found that the royal party would have to cross the Mersey by Sir John Butler's ferry, a passage that would not only cause many hours' delay, but which was not unaccompanied by danger, seeing the large number of horses and heavily laden sumpter mules. The Earl of Derby, therefore, being desirous of removing any possible inconvenience from the journey of his royal stepson, conceived the idea of building a bridge. He owned the land on the Cheshire side of the river, but was compelled to buy a piece of ground, belonging to one Norris of Warrington, on the Lancashire side. Immediately the purchase was effected he "builded a bridge at Warrington on both sides, being his own land", to the great disgust and annoyance of Sir John Butler, whose ferry was now rendered useless, and he himself deprived of the good income it had produced.

Sir John expressed his opinion of the Earl's action in building the bridge in no measured terms, and consequently a fierce quarrel broke out between the two. But when the King was approaching Warrington the Earl, apparently anxious to bring the quarrel to an end, sent a request to Sir John Butler that he should make one of the train of Lancashire noblemen and gentlemen who were accompanying him to meet the monarch. Sir John sent a contemptuous and most discourteous refusal.

The Earl of Derby—by reason of his relationship by marriage to Henry VII, and his vast possessions—was then all paramount in Lancashire, and such an affront to his high dignity could not be passed lightly by. Whether the Earl himself had any part in the dastardly means taken to avenge the insult is not known, but the name of his son, Lord Stanley, is given by the old chronicler as the instigator of the crime. "Sir John Butler, knt., was slaine in his bedde by the procurement of the Lord Standley, Sir Piers Leigh and Mister William Savage joining with him in that action".

The legend runs that, having bribed the porter at Bewsey Hall, the latter, in the dead of night, set a light in one of the windows to serve as a guide to the murderers across the broad moat, which they crossed in a "coracle", or leather boat.

> "What hideous thing comes swift and dark
>   Athwart that flickering wave?
> A spectre boat there seems to glide,
>   With many an uplift glaive.
>
> The bolts are unslid by that grim porter,
>   And a gladsome man was he
> When three foemen fierce strode up the stair
>   All trim and cautiously".

The traitorous porter led the three murderers to Sir John's sleeping chamber, but at the door they found his chamberlain, Houlcroft, guarding his master's slumbers. In vain they parleyed with him, but the faithful servant would not give them admission, and after a desperate resistance was hewn to the ground. The noise of the combat, the clashing of swords and the cries of the devoted Houlcroft had awakened Sir John, who, leaping from his bed, was fallen upon and hacked to pieces by the murderers before he could defend himself.

Lady Butler was sleeping in the same room, together with Sir John's infant son and heir. The miscreants spared her life, but having dispatched the father, rushed to the cradle with the intention of killing the child. Nothing less than the destruction of the line of Butler would apparently satisfy the Stanley vengeance for the affront put upon them by Sir John. But the cradle was empty.

Here there are two versions of the legend. One tells that whilst the murderers were occupied in their bloody work upon Houlcroft and his unfortunate master, a page passed through the porter's lodge carrying a basket. The wicked porter asks –

> "Now whither away, thou little page,
>   Now whither away so fast?
> 'They have slain Sir John', said the little page,
>   'And his head in this wicker cast'.
>
> 'And whither goest thou with that grisly head?'
>   Cried the grim porter again.
>   'To Warrington Bridge they bade me run,
> And set it up amain.'
>
> 'There may it hang', cried that loathly knave,
>   'And grin till its teeth be dry;
> While every day, with jeer and taunt,
>   Will I mock it till I die!'

It was not Sir John's head, however, that the page carried in his basket, but Sir John's child which, this version says, he conveyed "craftily" to the Priory of the

Hermit Friars of St Augustine near the bridge at Warrington, where it was recovered by the distracted mother on the following morning.

After vainly searching for the child the murderers descended the stairs, and discovered the trick played by the page upon the porter, whom they roundly accused of treachery –

> "They counted down the red, red gold;
>   And the porter laughed outright;
> Now we have paid thy service well
>   For thy master's blood this night;
>
> For the master's blood thou hast betrayed,
>   We've paid thee thy desire
> But for thy treachery unto us,
>   Thou hast not had thy hire".

Taking the porter with them across the moat, they hanged him—"they payed him a greate reward, and so coming away with him, they hanged him at a tree in Bewsey Parke".

The other version of the legend is the more credible of the two. This tells that a faithful negro servant, hearing the fray in Sir John's bedroom, rushed thither, and entering by a door opposite to that forced by the murderers, snatched up the infant from its cradle, and carried it to its nurse in an adjoining chamber. Returning to Sir John's bedroom, the negro held the three murderers at bay in the second doorway, while the nurse effected her escape with the child. Finally he, too, was killed, but in the meantime the child was safe at the Priory by Warrington Bridge. This story has proof which the other lacks, for on the alabaster tomb of Sir John and Lady Butler, in what was formerly the Bewsey Chapel in Warrington Church, is the figure of a negro, his body having been buried with those of his master and mistress as the last earthly reward that could be paid him for preserving the life of the infant heir. In the second version of the legend the traitorous porter is also hanged, after having been paid the blood money he demanded, but this was doubtless a precautionary measure on the part of the murderers, who would naturally wish to remove so damning and treacherous a witness to their crime and the deliberation with which it had been arranged.

Lady Butler commenced a prosecution against Sir John's murderers, but the machinery of the law in those days, especially when directed against a member of so powerful a family as the Stanleys, was not easily set in motion, and before her suit came on for hearing she had married Lord Grey, doubtless as a protection to herself and her child against her late husband's enemies. Her second husband, however, did not support her in her efforts to bring Sir John's murderers to justice, and exercising a right then existing he made her suit void. This, again, was probably due to Stanley influence. Whatever the reason, his wife did not submit tamely: "for which reason she parted from her husband and came into Lancashire, saying, 'If my lord will not let me have my will of my husband's enemies, yet shall my body be buried by him'. Forthwith the unhappy lady began to build the elaborate alabaster monument in Warrington Church, where in due time, she was buried beside her murdered husband and the faithful negro who had given his life in saving her child.

The descendants of Sir John continued to live at Bewsey Hall until 1603, when the estate was sold to the Irelands of Hale Hall.

Bewsey Hall is no more, but the bridge, which once had an Augustinian priory as a neighbour, played an important role during the Civil War. The Earl of Derby placed a garrison nearby to hold the bridge for Charles I but he failed to pursuade the town to raise the King's standard. Perhaps the elders supported Parliament, or more likely they were keeping their options open and staying neutral. Sir William Brereton arrived with a Parliamentary force and laid siege to the bridge, which at that time had an oratory over one of the centre spans once used by the Augustinian friars. The Earl of Derby threatened to set Warrington on fire rather than give in, and Sir William Brereton retired, but on 28th May, 1643, the bridge was taken by Colonel Ashton for Parliament, after a siege lasting five days. In 1745 the bridge was destroyed by the "Liverpool Blues" and other hastily mustered militia in order to prevent Bonnie Prince Charlie and his army from crossing the one and only bridge offering passage into Cheshire. In 1747 a new bridge was built for the town, and with modifications this bridge still serves Warrington well.

In 1795 J. Aitken published *A description of the Country from thirty to forty miles around Manchester*. After repeating the Bewsey Hall Legend, Aitken goes on to describe the Warrington of his day:

The principal part of the town consists of four streets crossing at the centre, one of which runs directly from the bridge and for its narrowness the mean buildings give an unfavourable idea of the place to a stranger. But some of the other streets are much opener and contain many good houses interspersed, the usual effect of commercial opulence rising in a place of antiquity. It has the common fault of being most straightened at the centre; a great inconvenience to a town which is one of the principal thoroughfares of the north, being the only entrance from the south to all the north western part of England, and the busy port of Liverpool. There is no bridge over the Mersey between Warrington and the sea and none for many miles upwards between it and Manchester. From this circumstance Warrington has always been a port of consequence in the civil commotions of this Kingdom, of which the most considerable was the slaughter and capture of a large body of the fugitive Scotch army under the Duke of Hamilton in 1648, after the defeat of the combined royal forces near Preston. Lambert was the parliamentary general on this occasion, who likewise made a stand here against the Scotch army which advanced under the young king in 1651, but was obliged to retreat. In the rebellion of 1745 the bridge at Warrington was broken down, whereby the Pretenders Army was induced to vary from their intended route Southwards and take the road through Manchester.

Warrington has long been of some note as a trading town. In the first part of this century a large quantity of coarse linens and checks was made in the town and neighbourhood, and sold at its markets; but in later years the manufacture of sail cloth or poldavy was introduced and raised to such a height that half the heavy sail

The Mersey at Warrington, with Warrington Bridge and the Academy reflected in its waters.

cloth used in the navy has been computed to be manufactured here. Sail cloth is for the most part made of hemp and flax mixed, but some is made of flax alone. The raw materials are chiefly brought from Russia to the port of Liverpool, whence they come to Warrington by water carriage. This manufacture has brought wealth and population to the place, but a branch of trade subject to such variation in the demand, according to the prevalence of peace or war, has had its inconveniences; and in fact Warrington has partaken less of the increased prosperity of the country than many other towns. During the interval between the last and the present war, several of the manufacturers exerted themselves to introduce the cotton branches here, and have succeeded to a considerable degree. As coarser cotton goods were those chiefly attempted, many of the sailcloth weavers, for the sake of more employment and better wages, turned to the new manufacture which caused a considerable decline of the old, but since the commencement of the war the use has been reversed. Various other trades have added to the business of the town. The making of pins has been, and still is, carried on to a pretty large extent; and locks, hinges and other articles of hardware are fabricated here. Large works for the smelting of copper was established near the town and used for several years, but have for some time been discontinued. The refining of sugar, and the making of glass have employed many hands; and the latter particularly is a flourishing branch of manufacture. An iron foundry has likewise been set up, which makes a variety of common articles. Warrington has long been noted for its malt and ale, and does pretty largely in the corn and flour trade. Besides these sources of gain and employment the great resort of travellers to the town promotes a considerable circulation of money. Its markets (the principal of which is on Wednesday, the other on Saturday) are frequented by an extensive and populous circumjacent country; though the Bridgewater Canal which passes a mile and a half to the south of Warrington in its course to Manchester has drawn off a good deal of business from this neighbourhood to the latter town.

Warrington may, in some measure be considered a port town, the Mersey admitting, by the help of tide vessels of seventy or eighty tons burthen to Bank Quay, a little below the Town, where Warehouses, Cranes and other conveniencis for landing goods are erected. The spring tides rise at the bridge to a height of more than nine feet. Upwards the river communication extends to Manchester. The Mersey naturally is well stocked with fish. In the proper seasons large quantities of salmon have been caught in the vicinity of the Town, so as formerly to afford a cheap article of food to the inhabitants; but the demands for the luxury of the great towns in its neighbourhood, and of the distant metropolis itself, together with a dimination of the number of fish owing to the frequent molestation and want of proper attention, having latterly made a rarity what was once a plentiful variety. The same may be said of the smelts and sparlings which annually in spring come up the river in Shoals formerly consisting of vast numbers and of a size superior to those of other parts. But both size and numbers have been much diminished as is supposed by the constant fishing in the lower parts of the river whereby the spawn and young fry are destroyed.

Warrington is well supplied with coals, partly by land carriage from the pits of Haydock and its neighbourhood, partly by the Sankey Canal which comes within a mile and a half of the town.

The land around Warrington consists of rich meadows bordering on the river, and occasionally flooded, and of pasture and garden ground. It is noted for its gooseberries which are superior in size, and a greater variety of kinds than in most parts of the Kingdom. A very fine kind of damson is also common here. Potatoes are raised in large quantities and thirty or forty thousand bushels have been shipped at Bank Quay in a year.

About thirty seven years since a seminary for educating youth upon a liberal academical plan was instituted in this town, and supported by subscriptions chiefly among the dissenters. It flourished during a considerable period under the care of tutors of eminence, but at length sunk through want of adequate support, and the difficulties of maintaining proper discipline.

This has something of a modern ring about it, despite being written nearly two hundred years ago, but there can be no doubting the brilliance of the one-time staff of the academy still standing near Warrington Bridge, and looking spruce after a facelift. Joseph Priestley, famous for his work towards the discovery of oxygen, taught here; and Manchester College, the interdenominational theological college at Oxford, evolved from the high-powered intellect of the tutors at Warrington Academy. John Harrison, reputed inventor of the marine chronometer, also worked here, and one of his apprentices, John Reinhold Forster, was appointed naturalist on Captain James Cook's second voyage.

Bank Hall, once the splendid home of the Patten family and whose iron gates were displayed at the Great Exhibition of 1851, has served as the Town Hall since 1872. Although changes have been made to allow it to function properly, the eighteenth century wall mouldings, chimney pieces, stone stairs and heavy doors remain. James Gibbs designed Bank Hall around 1750 and also had a hand in the design of Holy Trinity, a most imposing structure but not the oldest church in town. St. Elphin's is dominated by a high nineteenth century spire and the fourteenth century chancel below it shows signs of cannon balls fired by Cromwell's army as they took the town in 1648. A statue of Cromwell overlooks the bridge close to the Academy. Inside the church the theme is still a little violent, for here is the fifteenth century alabaster tomb of the murdered Sir John Butler. To cover Warrington's history would take more than a mere portion of a chapter; the reader should need no excuse to visit the museum on Bold Street or the public library, which in 1848 was the first in the country to be supported from the public rates.

The Mersey viewed from Warrington looks mucky, but as I stand on the bridge making the final notes for this chapter a redshank is feeding on the mud and further downstream a brave man is digging for worms with which to fish. Salmon have started to come up the Mersey and under the bridge, an event bound to make newspaper headlines for some time yet. But where there's life there's hope, and the Mersey is not half so sick as she was, although she takes a terrible beating between Warrington and the Runcorn Gap.

CHAPTER SEVEN

Warrington to the Runcorn Gap

A S WE HAVE seen, the River Mersey ceases to be navigable once Woolston Weir, some four miles above Warrington, is reached. For a while horse-drawn packet boats (the *Packet Boat Inn* still stands close to Warrington Bridge) carried passengers along the water to Manchester and other towns linked by the canal system. All other canal traffic had to give way to them, giving them the same reputation as inter-city trains have today. As roads improved, however, the stage coaches, able to reach smaller towns not on the canals, gradually became more popular than the packet boat, which was finally killed off as the railways developed.

The short stretch downriver to the Runcorn Gap has seen greater changes than any other reaches of the Mersey, and that is saying something. The Gap is only four hundred yards wide and an ideal place for a ferry and a bridge. In the old days only a ferry existed, the swirling waters of the river being so turbulent where they were funnelled through the gap that bridge supports could not be stabilised. The Runcorn Ferry was operating in the twelfth century, and the last ferryman named Harrison was still rowing his way to and fro in 1905. Since then the Runcorn Ferry has become something of a music hall joke, as one of Stanley Holloway's monologues shows.

> On the banks of the Mersey, over on Cheshire side,
> Lies Runcorn that's best known to fame
> By Transporter Bridge as tak's folks over its stream,
> Or else brings 'em back across same.
>
> In days afore Transporter Bridge were put up
> A ferry Boat lay in the slip,
> And old Ted the Boatman would row folks across
> At per tuppence per person per trip.

What has happened over the last century to the area between the Widnes-Runcorn gap and Warrington is best explained by taking an imaginary boat trip from Warrington Bridge, ending at Runcorn Docks. It should be stated clearly, though, that boating on this stretch can be a hazardous business as the currents can be very dangerous. The first tributary to be noticed is the Sankey Brook, which drains the area around St Helens. The town has extensive coal fields and since the eighteenth century has become world famous for its glass works, now owned by

Pilkingtons. Although Windleshaw Abbey, a fifteenth century chantry dedicated to St Helen, proves that there has been a settlement here for a long time, most of St Helens is modern and is there because of glass. The proximity of the alkali industry plus the even texture of the river sand stimulated the production of glass, the history of which is shown in Pilkington's museum on Prescot Road.

Sankey Brook Canal more or less follows the line of the brook and locks into the Mersey at Fiddlers Ferry, about three miles downstream from Warrington, the channel being marked by buoys.

In his book on the River Mersey published in 1944 W.T. Palmer described the ferry thus:

> a muddy but fairly large rowboat which plies from the stone jetty outside the Inn to some point on the Cheshire side. This is not identified by either farm or road access. The inn seems to be quite comfortable for visitors of a mildly adventurous mind. At night the sound of the tide must echo through the rooms, and in wind there will be resounding notes.

The ferry, now diesel powered, still carries workmen across the river to their work. At one time Fiddlers Ferry had pretentions as a shipbuilding area and in 1826 complaints were made by the shipbuilders Messrs Whidby, Giles and Rennie that the pier installations were causing

Looking across the Mersey from Widnes at the Fiddlers Ferry power station.

The launch of the three-masted schooner *Despatch* from Brunditt and Hayes' yard at Runcorn, from an old postcard.

serious silting in an area of the river already notoriously difficult to navigate.

By 1832 the problem of silting along the whole of this stretch had, if anything, worsened and this seriously interfered with the distribution of soap manufactured in increasing quantities at Warrington. River transport had the advantage of being cheap. This is perhaps why it was considered so necessary to keep the river from silting and why the scheme to build a railway bridge across the Mersey at Fiddlers Ferry in 1860 was vigorously opposed by George Crossfield, the largest soap producer in Warrington.

Perhaps in an effort to bring prosperity to Fiddlers Ferry, and with it the essential finance to keep the channel dredged, Thomas Wilkinson began to build ships here; between 1859 and 1885 sixteen ships were launched into the Mersey and three into the Sankey Canal. The river boats had one deck, one mast and were basically constructed of wood. The interesting feature of these Wilkinson vessels was their names, *Bream, Vendace, Carp, Brill, Rudd, Perch, Dace, Dab, Chub, Roach* and so on, all freshwater fish and highly appropriate for river boats.

During the eighteenth and nineteenth centuries the whole of the upper Mersey must have echoed to the sound of shipwrights working first in wood and then in iron. Vessels were built at Runcorn between

1778 and 1893, at Widnes from 1861 to 1890, at Frodsham from as early as 1728 to 1862. Between 1840 and 1857 twenty iron vessels were constructed at Warrington, three of them being paddle steamers, the *Warrington* (1843), the *Die Schoen Mainzen* (1845) and the *Invincible* (1852). Ships were also built at Sankey Bridges from 1807 until shipbuilding ended here in 1913, when the lightship *G.R. Jebb* eased her 69 tons into the river.

Just to the west of Fiddlers Ferry is an interesting hump known still as "Cromwell's Bank", which must have offered commanding views both of the ferry across the Mersey Gap and of troop movements in the vicinity of Warrington Bridge. Surely the astute generals of the Civil War must also have used a lookout post at Halton Castle, atop a knoll on the Cheshire side of the gap and also affording panoramic views all the way to Warrington.

The once magnificent old castle and the attractive new church together on a red sandstone bluff survey the scene below. The river itself and the ship canal shine like ribbons, reflecting every ray of sunshine. The castle was built by the Norman Barons of Halton soon after the Conquest, no doubt to subdue the rebellious natives. Things were still a bit unruly when *Piers Plowman* was written in the fourteenth century, as the following verse in its quaint style shows:

Thoro the pass of Haltoun
Poverte might passe whith owte peril of robbyrye

From its building the castle was put to many uses. It was one of the many residences to pass into the hands of the mighty John of Gaunt, who used it mainly as a hunting lodge. When his son Bolingbroke became King Edward I Halton was absorbed into the lands of the Duchy of Lancaster and by 1579 it was serving as a prison for recusants—catholics who refused to accept Henry VIII as the head of the English Church. What dreadful scenes of torment and torture must have been enacted within these now-ruined walls.

By virtue of its position and the thickness of its walls the castle must have been one of the most secure in all England, until the arrival of artillery. It was Sir William Brereton's "field pieces" which overcame the Royalist garrison in 1643. Brereton withdrew when Prince Rupert entered the district, but the Parliamentary forces returned and at the end of the war the castle was dismantled. The Parliamentarians then sold the ruined castle to Henry Brook, but after the Restoration in 1660 it reverted to the Crown.

Halton has two very tangible relics which take us back over the centuries. At one time the Lord of the Castle had wide legal powers over a great deal of Chester and parts of Lancashire on the other side of the river. From 1347 the Court Leet records were meticulously kept, and these make fascinating reading. In 1380 William Harper had to make the nerve-jangling journey all the way from Chester just to be hanged, since there was a custom in those days that criminals were hung in chains as close as possible to the scene of the crime. In 1474 two Welshmen were hanged for burglary at Keckwich. The court also dealt with more trivial matters; in 1655 a man was fined for allowing his wife "to fight and draw blood". In addition the Court Leet acted as the local weights and measures office, and it is a fair bet that the officials took it in turns to "taste ale". Only the muscular ones would be willing to enforce the law which penalised those who loitered more than one hour in an alehouse! Bakers, buttermakers and tanners were all subject to the all-seeing eye of the Court Leet official; who said that red tape was a purely modern hazard?

Halton's most interesting and unusual possession has been its unique library, founded in 1733 and supported by a then substantial annual grant of £12 per year by Sir John Chessyre. A Greek-style porch to get the reader off to a good start, a magnificently panelled room and an inventory of over four hundred books recorded on vellum made this library the envy of the country. In 1849 there were still only 422 books, and it therefore seems that the initial momentum was not maintained. Perhaps thinking was befuddled by the smothering influence of eye-watering fumes produced by the developing alkali industry based on Runcorn and Widnes.

Once a health resort sporting the name of Montpelier, Runcorn is often assumed to have had no existence before the nineteenth century. There is, however, evidence to support the contention that a castle at Runcorn was founded in AD 915 by King Alfred's daughter Aethelfleda, but all remains of this were apparently removed during the hectic period of canal and railway building, when there was no time to consider historic piles of rock. There is no doubt why the Mercian princess should have built a fortress in the Mersey gap; it gave her an ideal defensive position from which to repel the boats of the Danes. A Christian church was in operation when the Normans came and Nigel, the Baron of Halton, who probably came over the sea with William I, placed his own priest, one named Wolfaith, in charge. From his name it does sound as if Wolfaith was a Saxon, and Nigel may have made a "political appointment". William FitzNigel, the second Baron, established an Augustinian house at Runcorn in 1115 but their stay was a short one, the brethren moving to Norton in 1134.

Although Halton was the more important settlement it must have looked to the river at its feet for trade and the use of Runcorn as its port must have been vital. Whatever the reason for its success, Runcorn was doing well enough in 1481 for Chester to appeal to Edward IV, who happened also to be the Earl of Chester, to do something about the upstart which was taking away their trade. Henry reacted by ordering the Mayor of Dublin not to deal with any port in Cheshire except Chester. Any vessel unwise enough not to comply was to be arrested. This worked, Chester flourished and by 1540 Runcorn was almost deserted, remaining isolated until the late seventeenth century when industry on the Mersey began to develop, a trend which accelerated at an almost unbelievable rate during the eighteenth and especially the nineteenth century.

The Sankey Canal certainly provided a much-needed boost to Runcorn, but its real heyday was to come as a result of the building of the Bridgewater Canal and also the Old Quay Canal linking Warrington and Runcorn. Between 1801 and 1847 the population of Runcorn increased fourfold and it became a port in its own right independent of Liverpool. In fact Liverpool's own development owed something to Runcorn, many of its new buildings being constructed from red sandstone blocks cut from Runcorn quarries and shipped downriver. In 1850 Runcorn had declined a little and was brought back into the fold of the Port of Liverpool, but by 1862 it was back on its feet and independent once more. A giant dockland complex had its eye on the gap, however, and when the ship canal was finished Runcorn, albeit reluctantly, became integrated into the Port of Manchester.

The canal has proved something of a mixed blessing to Runcorn. While the canal was under construction employment boomed, the population temporarily increased and alehouses echoed to the sound of navvies laughing, fighting and competing for the favours of painted ladies. Shipbuilding yards were cut off from deep water by the canal wall, but there was some switch of labour to the construction of canal vessels in the "sprinch" yard* at the Big Pool. The Old Quay, however, with its huge six-storey flour mill on the edge of the Runcorn to Latchford Canal, was in the way of the brash, confident ship canal and down everything came. Again, alternative jobs were available since the canal allowed the passage of huge ships from Eastham to Manchester, the only vessels not being able to pass being those whose masts would not pass beneath the railway bridge. The Mersey had already been spanned in 1845 when the Runcorn Gap and St Helens Railway Company's massively impressive bridge allowed Lancashire coal to pass into Cheshire, while salt was carried on the return trip. Eventually the transporter bridge, an amazing feat of engineering, carried road traffic over both the ship canal and the

---

*A "sprinch" yard is a local term used to describe a yard building canal boats rather than seagoing craft.

Mersey. An equally impressive road bridge opened in 1961 now spans the same gap and the transporter bridge has been demolished.

So it is that the green fields alongside the Mersey which delighted picnickers during the last century are now swamped beneath one of the greatest concentrations of industry in the world. This ensures the future of Runcorn docks, although in these days of container traffic it does not necessarily safeguard very many jobs.

The Alkali Industry

Runcorn and Widnes have been at the centre of the Industrial Revolution, which depends so heavily on alkali, for over a century. You cannot make soap or glass without liberal quantities of alkali, and this must obviously be produced as cheaply as possible. Neither can textiles be properly finished without alkali.

The bridge linking Runcorn and Widnes.

Smoke over Widnes, 1895, from an old photograph in the archives of the Halton Chemical Industry Museum at Widnes.

In the early days alkali could only be produced by the backbreaking business of collecting seaweed or vast quantities of bracken or wood, a diminishing asset in the eighteenth century, and burning it to an ash which contained the vital sodium or potassium salts. Then came a breakthrough by a French chemist, Leblanc, whose process revolutionised alkali production. Those who had to work in it faced conditions worse, in my opinion, than those in any other industry. Heaven knows how the human body stood up to it, but stand up to it the workers did, and in doing so made their masters rich.

Leblanc's process involved two stages. In the first salt was mixed with sulphuric acid and, with much evil bubbling, salt cake (sodium sulphate) was formed. Hydrochloric acid gas steamed off into the atmosphere and into eyes and lungs. The salt cake was then removed and heated in a furnace after limestone and coal had been added. More stench, smoke and choking fumes belched out into the atmosphere until only a black ash remained. This was then dropped into huge tanks of water, producing a solution which was used to produce soda crystals or soda ash, which could be further converted into caustic soda (sodium hydroxide), the alkali demanded by industry in vast quantities.

But at what cost? A high one indeed. Was it worth the virtual rape of the countryside around the Mersey Gap? The answer must be a reluctant yes. What was needed was some control over the polluting effects of the industry, the hydrochloric acid in the atmosphere being particularly

113

damaging. Acid rain is by no means an invention of twentieth-century conservationists. Add to this the burning of over 130 million tons of coal every year around the Mersey gap at the end of the nineteenth century and you begin to see the problem.

As early as 1863 the passing of a number of Alkali Acts represented an attempt to tackle the problem. The dumping of toxic waste is not just a twentieth-century problem either, and the oozing "galligoo", named after the noise it made when dumped at the end of the Leblanc process, presented a real problem. As rainwater slowly dissolved this waste and carried it into the streams and onwards into the Mersey, hydrogen sulphide was produced. The concentration of this rotten-egg gas was so high that streams often burst spontaneously into flames. What a terrible environment in which to live. Eventually a method of rendering the Leblanc waste less lethal was developed, and then in 1873 the invention of the Solvay process brought a way of producing better, safer alkali; the first nail was driven into the coffin of the Leblanc process.

The Leblanc process survived because of the recovery of hydrochloric acid from its salt cake; reacting this with manganese dioxide—another hazardous process—produced bleaching powder. This was eagerly sought by the textile and papermaking industries, especially those along the Irwell and the Croal. Just before the advent of the twentieth century an American chemist named Castner developed a process of extracting chlorine direct from brine, which meant the end of the Leblanc process (not before time) and the beginning of a boom period for the Cheshire salt lakes along the Weaver valley, as described in the next chapter.

An aerial view of Spike Island, with the chimney of Gossage's soap works in a central position. The buildings have now gone and been replaced by a tree-lined conservation area. *Halton Chemical Industry Museum*

The Widnes/Runcorn area has other chemical industries besides alkali, and in its time has produced copper and copper sulphate, steel alloys, and recently the flourine-based chemicals used as refrigerants and as aerosol propellants. It is the chlorine-based industries which have, however, typified the area and are still important today. Thermoplastics, PVC, dry cleaning fluids and protective paints are now produced in vast quantities, and although they do produce pollution it is by no means as bad as in the past; voluntary controls are often devised by the companies themselves. We who complain about, but do not work in, these places should remember that we need their products and would be the first to complain if essential production ceased.

Very little of the old alkali industry remains, but it is pleasing to see that efforts are being made to set up an alkali museum in the Halton area. Those of us who love the Mersey should aim to preserve her natural history and at the same time pay homage to the less attractive parts of her history.

This chapter seems to have concentrated rather heavily on the Cheshire side of the river, tending to ignore Widnes on the Lancashire side. Let us not bother with the bridge and instead cross, in our imagination, the old ferry which it is said was begun or perhaps continued by John, sixth Baron of Halton, in 1178. He gave land on either side of the river to the Order of Knight Hospitallers on condition that they provided a free ferry. When the Baron died on the Crusade of 1190 the Prior of the Hospitallers gave land to Richard de la More, who was to continue to run the ferry "for the love of God".

Widnes gets its name from two Norse words, Vide and Ness, meaning Wide Nose, referring to the widening of the Mersey just before the Runcorn gap. The widest point is very sheltered, and Spike Island was produced when the St Helens Canal isolated land between canal and river. "Spike" was a dialect word for the doss houses which sprang up as workers moved in to work at Gossage's soap works. The area must at that time have been more polluted than anywhere in Britain; workers' teeth fell out and their lungs were shattered by fumes.

In recent years the old buildings have been demolished and the area intelligently landscaped. A fishing fleet is based at the canal basin, passing out into the river on the high tide to catch shrimps and flatfish.

Described as "a quiet industrial village" around 1860, Widnes has built ships, belched smoke, acidified the air, worked hard and increased its population. Clean Air Acts and improved industrial techniques have given Widnes an improved image in recent years, a compliment which applies equally to the towns and villages on the both banks of the Mersey as it widens from the Runcorn gap and heads seawards.

CHAPTER EIGHT

The River of Salt—The Weaver

VISIT THE grand old village of Frodsham and climb the steep winding road to Mersey View. Here is a modern restaurant and a small snack bar surrounded by a spacious picnic area set on a breezy bluff of sandstone plunging sheer to the village below. Walk from the spacious car park to the war memorial on the summit and look down to the right at the splendid old parish church, while straight in front and below, spread out like a map, is the River Weaver and its navigation winding towards the Manchester Ship Canal and the Mersey. Away to the left and capped by a smudge of smoke is the Stanlow refinery.

Even allowing for the fact that at Widnes and Runcorn are some of the country's heaviest industries, I know of no finer sight than this, especially at night when the twinkle of lights from house, hostelry, ship, factory, road, rail and bridge reflect from the waters of two substantial rivers and what was once one of the world's mightiest canal enterprises. In the daytime birds such as yellowhammers, greenfinches and stonechats flit between the fringing hawthorn and broom, which in summer paints the headland with a glorious blaze of yellow. A cuckoo often mingles its call in the month of June with the trill of an ascending lark and the deep rumble of a ship on passage to or from the I.C.I. complexes.

Over the last two hundred years or so the Weaver has given its life to the salt trade. To begin our study of the river we will need to come down from our lofty perch on Mersey View and look at Frodsham and Weston villages, sited on either side of the Weaver as it merges into the ship canal and the Mersey. Let us also look at the Weaver bends, an area rightly famous in the ornithological world, before continuing upstream to Weaverham and Northwich, with its famous Anderton lift, to its junction with the River Dane, and to its birthplace high in the Peckforton hills.

Any industry depends upon good transport, and salt is no exception. To the traders of ancient Britain Northwich was Heledd Dhu, which means the black salt town, while Nantwich was called Hellath wen, the white salt town. Even today traces of the old salt roads leading from the brine springs can be traced from Cheshire, many being strengthened by the Romans for military as well as commercial reasons. This was the case with Watling Street which linked York, Manchester, Chester and London. The road (the present A49) passed through Northwich, and there is little doubt that salt was transported along it. Another important salt town in Roman times was Middlewich, appropriately named by the Romans Salinae, which was fed by King Street which ran from Wilderspool (Warrington). Although it has not been proved with certainty, it seems to me that there must have been a linking road between King Street and Watling Street. Salt was still being exported via a land route from the valley of the River Weaver at the time of the Domesday Book, and an entry in this makes it abundantly clear that salt was a valuable commodity and in every sense of the word rationed. A tax was payable on salt, and the entry in Domesday shows how seriously the authorities treated attempts at evasion:

> Whoever loaded his wain so that the axle broke within a league of either wich gave ii shillings to the King's or the Earl's officer, if he were overtaken within the league. In like manner, he who loaded his horse, so as to break its back, gave ii shillings if overtaken within the league, but nothing if overtaken beyond it. Whoever made two horse loads out of one was found xl shillings if the officer overtook him.

A look at an O.S. map often reveals the old salt roads, and names like Salterswell, Salterford, Salthouses and Saltersford are self-explanatory. The Weaver dodges in and out of two of the three wiches, but until the eighteenth century was not used by salt manufacturers for transport. Until the Industrial Revolution the villages along the Weaver, although

Looking across the Mersey from Frodsham Hill, with the Rocksavage chemical works and the Manchester Ship Canal in the centre. The River Weaver can be seen at right entering the Mersey.

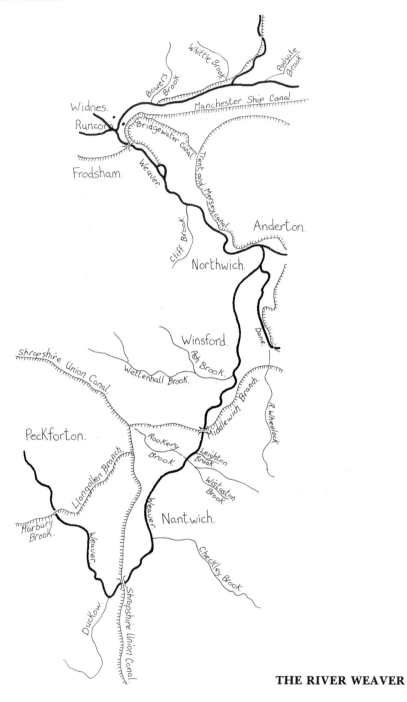

THE RIVER WEAVER

producing salt on a limited scale, were largely undisturbed by the throb of commerce. By the time the seventeenth century came to its conclusion new salt deposits were being discovered and mining techniques developed, and this resulted in a demand to make the Weaver navigable above Frodsham Bridge. Prior to this a slow and therefore relatively expensive trail led to Frodsham docks.

Strange as it may seem, the main objectors to the Weaver navigation scheme were the short-sighted salt manufacturers themselves, who thought that it would make salt cheaper without any benefit to themselves. What it did do was to provide a cheap route for coal to fuel the boilers in which the brine was evaporated to produce salt. Despite this opposition, and that from local fishermen, the scheme took shape from 1721 onwards, resulting in the construction of a dozen locks between Winsford and Frodsham. Thus the meandering Weaver was straightened so rigidly that it is more reminiscent of a canal than of a river. The Frodsham marshes, however, were never completely conquered and a deep canal was cut to link with the Mersey at Weston Point, a major dock being constructed by 1810. Several other cuts, including the Manchester Ship Canal and the Trent and Mersey, built to connect the Potteries with Liverpool and its export potential, criss-cross the area, and today the whole length of the Weaver navigation is a riot of actual and reflected colour as pleasure craft cruise gently through the lush Cheshire countryside.

The reason for the richness of the Cheshire salt deposits has caused some debate in geological circles. Salt may be obtained either as liquid brine or as solid rock salt, usually called halite from the Greek word for salt, hels. Whenever there is a shallow sea and a hot sun to evaporate the water, salt deposits will be laid down and become folded into the earth's crust during its movements over a long period of time. The areas of what is now Cheshire and Worcestershire where salt occurs were, during the Triassic period (about 200 million years ago), washed by a shallow sea and scorched by a blazing tropical sun. In 1912 Sir Thomas Hollan suggested that this area had extensive salt flats into which the sea ebbed and flowed; puddles left behind were like gigantic salt pans in which deposits built up layer by layer over the centuries. In later ages water seeping below ground dissolved these deposits to produce brine some eight times more concentrated than sea water; these underground reservoirs were occasionally crushed by hundreds of feet of impermeable rock and squeezed dry to produce rock salt, which we now obtain by mining.

Salt is a compound made up of an atom of sodium and an atom of chlorine held together by the attraction of opposite electric charges, positive on the sodium and negative on the chlorine. This is why sodium chloride can be split by the application of a powerful electric current. Liquid sodium, which melts at 98°C, is used as a coolant in nuclear reactors and extracts heat because being a metal it is an excellent thermal conductor. Sodium is also added to petrol as the so called anti-knock additive, helping engines to run more smoothly. Sodium hydroxide is also the basic material for the production of washing soda and soap.

Apart from its controversial use as a poison gas in the trench war of 1914-1918 and its acceptable use as a germ killer in swimming baths, chlorine has many uses in industry, including bleaching wood pulp for the paper industry. It can be employed for bleaching cotton but not wool, which is too delicate to be subjected to chlorine. The acidic gas is also used as the basis for producing carbon tetrachloride, a dangerous chemical used in dry cleaning, as well as chloroform, explosives, D.D.T. (dichlorodiphenyltrichloroethane) and in paints and plastics, especially PVC (Polyvinylchloride). As research goes on the lists tend to lengthen rather than shorten, and the demand for sodium and chlorine increase.

Around the salt-river are many complex industrial plants labelled Castner Kelner, after the inventors of the process which by passing massive electrical currents through brine produces sodium hydroxide (from which sodium is extracted) and chlorine, delivering them separately. Brine is also used in the manufacture of sodium carbonate by the Solvay process.

The significance of sodium carbonate in the modern world is profound, some thirty-five per cent of the product being absorbed by the glass industry. It is no accident that Pilkington's massive glass factory is sited at St Helens, within easy reach of Cheshire brine. A further seventeen per cent is used in washing and bleaching textiles and ten per cent used in soap manufacture, another important industry on the banks of the Mersey, for which the Weaver is once more a vital feeder artery. The paper industry takes another ten per cent and other uses are in the manufacture of sodium silicate (water glass), borax, and water softening chemicals.

Brine extraction was known long before mining began, and the Romans quickly learned, no doubt from the ancient Britons brought under their yoke, the position of the brine springs, especially those at Middlewich. The precise mechanism of extraction they used is not clear, but William Camden's survey of late sixteenth century Britain mentions both Nantwich and Northwich, the latter's salt well being described as "a deep and plentiful brine pit with stairs under it, by which, when they have drawn the water in their leather buckets, they ascend half naked to the troughs to fill them".

The production of salt by the open pan process seen in a series of photographs from the Salt Museum, Northwich. Here wallers are using long-handled rakes to draw the salt to the side of the pan.

Loading common salt from the hurdles on which it has been laid to dry.

A lumpman turning out the salt lumps formed at a later stage of the refining process.

Cheshire Libraries and Museums

The brine was then evaporated and the salt left behind was marketed. No one then knew the precise source of this rich bounty, and it was only after rock salt was discovered in 1670 that folk realised where the brine originated. As knowledge of pump mechanisms developed brine was pumped to the surface. An interesting reference to the early use of a pump occurs in the writings of the fifth Earl of Huntington, who in 1636 visited Nantwich:

> They set pumps within a pit within a yard of the bottom, which they pump into a cistern or reserve, from which it runs through troughs of wood, which are both narrow and shallow, into 55 houses where they boil it to salt, taking the water with a bucket out of a cistern and putting it into great square pans of lead.

By the beginning of the nineteenth century windmills, water wheels and horses were being used to power the pumps, and the firm of Salmon and Penlingron were experimenting with a Boulton and Watt steam engine as early as 1799.

Sinking a shaft to tap the brine deposits was a hazardous operation. The liquid is under considerable pressure, and when the tough cap of marlstone called the flag is pierced the brine spurts out and the ground above eventually sinks. This has caused the Cheshire flashes, which are such a haven for waterfowl, and is also responsible for the quaint twisted and leaning buildings so typical of towns along the Weaver valley, especially Northwich. The problem of subsidence was increased after many small firms amalgamated to form the Salt Union of 1888 and the demand for brine accelerated.

In 1911 the union (of employers, not workers) laid on a pipeline to deliver "bastard" brine from mid-Cheshire to the salt works at Weston Point, thus cutting transport costs, but the extravagant demands of an increasingly important alkali industry caused subsidence on a massive and dangerous scale along the ill-used Weaver valley. Natural brine extraction has now thankfully been replaced by a system of controlled brine pumping devised by I.C.I. in which water is forced down a steel-lined borehole right into the salt bed, dissolving the salt and forcing the resulting brine to the surface; measured amounts can be taken, and the borehole is discontinued when sufficient brine has been extracted, a substantial layer of rock being left above it to prevent subsidence. So far this system seems to have worked admirably.

From the time that John Jackson discovered rock salt at Northwich in 1670 while searching for coal for landowner William Marbury (his lands now form part of an excellent country park), the Cheshire workers have been classified as "salt men" and "rock men". The earliest use for the mined rock salt was in the strengthening of the brine. A great deal of unco-ordinated, ill-considered and at times almost suicidal mining went on as the demand for salt increased, yet there is still sufficient to last for thousands of years.

In 1946 I.C.I. estimated that some seventy-eight pits were still working, but brine now meets all demands made by industry, although our increasing dependence upon road transport demands constant supplies of salt to help melt ice on the carriageways. The one remaining highly mechanised mine at Winsford produces two and a quarter million tons of salt per annum, quite sufficient to satisfy the demand for road salt throughout Britain. The next time you drive along a snow-slushed winter

Small tortoiseshell butterflies blow around like confetti on the banks of the River Weaver.

road, spare a thought for the valley of the Weaver, its lovely towns and villages bent and twisted in the service of mankind.

This chapter, which began on the breezy ozone-filled heights of Mersey View, can best be concluded by descending into Frodsham and tracing the Weaver back to its source. Crossing the bridge over the Weaver into Frodsham and looking seawards brings the feeling not of an industrial river but of a clear wide stream where yachts tack against the breeze and slip under one bridge carrying the railway and another supporting the M55 motorway. Beyond, the river winds through the marshes and slips into the ship canal. A delightful main street hewn out of solid rock is lined by old inns, some having spacious yards once the scene of Dickensian-like hubbub as stage coaches went about their business. The shops and houses are a strange amalgam of black half timbering and white plaster, thatching and slating. Historians will find the church with its late fourteenth century tower and twelfth century arcades and clerestory impressive both in dimensions and atmosphere. The gargoyles squint outwards from their lairs on the walls over the ship canal to the Mersey at a view almost as panoramic as that from Mersey View, which hangs over the church.

Naturalists visiting Frodsham are sure of a big surprise, whether they go down to the woods at Delamere or venture where the Weaver bends. Delamere Forest is five miles from Frodsham and well signed; the name means The Forest of the Meres. A substantial portion is under the coniferous blanket of the Forestry Commission, but since 1968 the combined expertise of the Cheshire County Council and the Commission has produced excellent picnic sites and leisurely walks have been signed through the trees.

Bird life in coniferous woodland is not so sparse as is often inferred, and in winter crossbills feed on the seeds in the cones, while in summer green woodpeckers and jays are sometimes seen apparently dancing on the nests of the wood ant, which are constructed from huge piles of conifer needles. They do this deliberately to annoy the ants, which spray formic acid on to the birds' plumage and thus destroy feather lice—a sort

The Island Church at Weston Docks, which lies between the Mersey, the Manchester Ship Canal and the docks themselves, was built to serve the watermen using the Weaver Navigation.

of ornithological aerosol known to the bird-folk as "anting". In the case of the green woodpecker with its long sticky tongue the wood ant is an important item of diet, and the presence of new conifer plantations may well account for the increasing range firstly of the wood ant and secondly of the green woodpecker which depends upon it.

On my last visit to Frodsham during June, 1984, I followed the appropriately named Marsh Lane and found it to be full of "birders", a peculiar breed of ornithologist who race from one end of Britain to the other in search of rarities to add to their list of species seen; "Twitchers"

The caterpillar of the large cabbage white.
Robert Howe

is another name for them. On this occasion they were all hotfoot in pursuit of a shy stilt sandpiper in full breeding plumage, apparently blown off course during its springtime movements through North America. More common birds, however, abound. Herons fish in the shallows and along the edges of the flood plain fields, criss-crossed with drainage ditches, while behind them tower the cranes, warehouses and chemical complexes around the village of Weston.

One can stand on the tiny village green at Weston, dominated by the recently restored medieval market cross, and look down at the dock complex. Towering over the harbour installations is the spire of Christ Church, otherwise known as the Island Church, originally built with several others along the Weaver Navigation so that the busy boatmen did not fail to pray for a good wind. All the others save this one on Weston Point have been demolished. There is a right of access to the church via a narrow passage opposite the post office, but this has been closed by agreement with I.C.I for security reasons and churchgoers are admitted via a manned barrier. Around the church a few rhododendrons have been planted, and bird-sown hawthorn, birdsfoot trefoil, bramble, weld, valerian and a host of other colourful and nectar-full flowers grow on the dock side to attract butterflies which blow like confetti in the breeze. Common species here include the common blue, green veined and cabbage whites, small tortoiseshell, meadow brown, wall brown and grayling.

The smell of salt is everywhere, and its heady scent easily reaches the old village perched on the headland, which has its own church built as a result of an appeal of a unique nature. The parish church of St John the Evangelist was built around 1898 as a result of a series of letters written by the choirboys of the former church to prominent local businessmen— the salt of the earth, so to speak. The delightfully spacious and airy building quite properly has a plaque close to the altar proclaiming the noble efforts of the choirboys; we must hope that their voices were as high and as clear as their convictions. The religious building it replaced still stands but dates back only to 1863, when Major George Orred, who had inherited the land of the late Anne Orred and the manorial rights of Weston, gave a plot of land and £500 towards the building of a mission in Weston. Under the leadership of Canon Barclay, the then vicar of Runcorn, the Anglicans of Weston raised the balance needed to erect a dual-purpose building to serve as a school and a church dedicated to St John the Evangelist, probably because Anne Orred's birthday fell on St John's Day, 27th December. It is interesting that the first donation received by the choirboys was one from John Cavendish Orred. The school closed in 1968, but the old mission still serves as a Sunday school and as a base for a playgroup.

The village has some interesting old buildings, including Cavendish Farm dated 1628, Manor Farm, 1625, and the Old Hall built in 1607. The view from Weston Point is still magnificent, the silver ribbon of the widening Mersey twinkling across the narrow strips of ship canal and Weaver. The Wirral peninsular is easily seen, as are the Welsh hills, and a strange compelling atmosphere surrounds the Castner Kellner North and South Works, which are the largest generators of chlorine in Europe. Here, too, is the terminus of the pipeline bringing brine from central Cheshire to the electrolytic works of I.C.I. There can be no finer example than the Weaver of how a river can absorb industry and stay relatively pretty; to follow it inland takes you through some of the greenest and most fertile land in all England. The industrialised towns are few, and small enough not to dominate the river completely.

An old Saxon salt town cradled in a fold of the Weaver, Weaverham has attractive timbered houses and some thatched dwellings surrounded by old English cottage gardens. Despite a little modern building, time has dealt kindly both with the village and with its splendid parish church

The River Dane at Holmes Chapel, Cheshire.

dedicated to St. Mary the Virgin. An earlier church warranted an entry in the Domesday Book of 1086: "There is a church and a priest here, and a mill to serve the hall".

In fact there have been three churches at Weaverham, all probably on the same site. There was a substantial Saxon church recorded in the reign of Edward I (1272-1307) as under the control of the monks of nearby Vale Royal Abbey, of which no trace now remains. It seems fairly certain that the village supplied the monks with their salt. The construction of the second church began in 1281 and was complete by 1360; the present building dates from the fifteenth century, but apart from the tower most of the structure is sixteenth century.

At Northwich the River Dane adds its considerable volume of water to the Weaver, the two meeting close to the town centre, through which runs Watling Street. Many of the buildings look as if they have been struck by an earthquake, but this is no act of God but an act of man greedy for salt. Just around the corner from the city centre is a building labelled "Cheshire Brine Compensation Board", ample proof that the town tends to sink into the holes left by the extracted brine. Some buildings are propped, others lifted, but they are all worth saving, for you get the feeling of being in an Austrian or Swiss Alpine village as you wander around the black and white timbered buildings with their gables and fronts lavishly decorated with brightly painted wooden figures. There is a cheerful cavalier on a bank and nearby is a town crier with his bell and a watchman with his lantern; a man accompanied by his wife, plus mugs of ale, looks for all the world like a huge toby jug.

The student of salt in general and the Weaver in particular would do well to visit the Salt Museum in the Weaver Hall in London Road, Northwich. For a modest fee you can relax in the comfort of a lecture theatre and enjoy an audio visual slide show describing the history of salt and its associated industries. Imaginative exhibits show how salt was mined, how the various chemical processes including the Castner-Kellner process work, the social conditions of other times and the types of sailing and steam vessels employed on the Weaver navigation.

Many leaflets can be purchased, including one on the Anderton boat lift, one of the wonders of the engineering age. To appreciate the sheer magnitude of this astounding mechanical marvel which lifts boats from the Weaver to the canal fifty feet above, one must pay a visit, or better still take a pleasure cruiser and be lifted with it from river to canal. At the moment of writing (July, 1984), however, fears are growing that the lift, closed since the autumn, will never reopen. Corrosion in the main

supports means that expensive repairs will be needed, and, as a British Waterways spokesman told the *Manchester Evening News*, "there is no early prospect of reopening. It is suffering from old age. The question is how far we can go on repairs".

The lift had its origins rather more than a hundred years ago in the increasing trade being pushed along the Trent and Mersey Canal, particularly pottery from Staffordshire to Liverpool, the smooth-water passage being so much more economic than the jolting clank and rattle of packhorse. The Weaver is fifty feet below the canal and goods had either to be physically humped between the two or shot down a wooden shute. Because of a shortage of water an extensive locking system linking the two was not entirely satisfactory and a structure less demanding of water was required. Necessity proved to be the mother of invention, as ever, and river engineer Edward Leader Williams came up with an ambitious, and to some an outrageous, plan for a cast and wrought-iron lift with huge tanks in which barges and narrowboats could float as they were raised and lowered. Each tank measured a staggering 75 feet by 15 feet by 5 feet. To connect the canal with the upper level of the lift a huge aqueduct 162 feet long was constructed. From its opening in 1875 the lift worked on a hydraulic system involving pumping water into the upper tank, thus increasing its weight and pulling up the lower tank and boats

The Anderton boat lift, opened in 1875 to convey loaded canal craft from the River Weaver to the Trent and Mersey Canal fifty feet above. The diagram on the right shows how this wonder of nineteenth-century engineering worked.

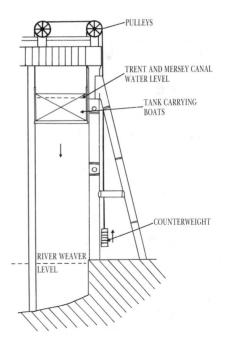

PULLEYS

TRENT AND MERSEY CANAL
WATER LEVEL

TANK CARRYING
BOATS

COUNTERWEIGHT

RIVER WEAVER
LEVEL

from the Weaver, the drop being controlled by ingenious gearing mechanisms. A major overhaul and substantial design modifications involving pulleys and cogs was carried out in 1908, and we must hope that the engineers and financiers of the 1980s are just as resourceful as their counterparts a century ago. We cannot afford to allow one of the greatest achievements of the canal age to rust away; it deserves preservation, if for no other reason than its potential tourist attraction.

There are picnic benches, extensive areas of grass and viewing platforms all around the lift, and steep tree-fringed steps descend to the Anderton basin on the Weaver. Commercial vessels have not ventured into the lift for a number of years, but there is still a future for it due to the ever-increasing number of pleasure craft using Britain's inland waterways.

Before following the course of Northwich's other river, the Dane, let us continue along the Weaver through Winsford, Nantwich, Audlem, Cholmondeley and up to the sheep farms around the Peckforton Hills to the north west.

Despite extensive salt works the Weaver at Winsford looks surpri-

The flat *Eustace Carey*, typical of the sailing craft used on the Mersey and on the Weaver Navigation to carry cargoes of salt and other goods.
Halton Chemical Industry Museum.

singly clear, its course widened into still pools which reflect the colourful sails of yachts and the clear lines of small motor-cruisers. The two settlements which made up Winsford, Wharton and Over, are separated by the river, having been large enough in 1086 to warrant a significant entry in the Domesday Book. Its tranquil old English calm has been retained in some parts despite the industry and its increasing use by both Liverpool and Manchester as overspill areas, requiring housing of all shapes, sizes and budgets. When we consider that the Weaver and its many tributaries drain some 870 square miles of rich Cheshire farmland and that eighty-three sewage works discharge effluent into it, the river must have great resistance. Some settlement occurs in Winsford flashes, which is an area rich in birdlife. The quality of the Weaver can vary from Class 1 to Class 4 but is mostly in the 2 to 3 range.

Apart from salt, Nantwich has been famed for its rich Cheshire cheese and for the exploits of its greatest son, John Gerard, the renowned writer of the *Herbal and General Historie of Plants* during the time of Elizabeth I, who was in charge of Lord Burghley's gardens in the Strand as well as having his own physic garden in London. Some of Gerard's herbal has the distinct flavour of quackery about it, but much of it has succeeded in distilling the essence of a countryman's knowledge of useful plants; it is rightly regarded as one of the best texts in scientific botany of the period. Here and there a spark of northern humour shines through:

> The roote of Solomon's Seale taketh away in one night or two at the most any Bruise, black or blewe spots, gotten by falls or Women's wilfullness in stumbling upon their hasty Husbande's Fistes

Nantwich has still retained some of the quaint twisting charm and beauty which Gerard would recognise. Nantwich suffered a fire during the reign of Elizabeth I of such magnitude that the monarch herself contributed to the disaster fund. I wonder if Gerard himself communicated the disaster to his queen, but in any event her generosity was commemorated in an inscription on a house built by Thomas Clees which reads:

> God grant our Royal Queen
> In England long to reign
> For she has put her helping hand
> To build this town again.

The grand old church not only survived the fire but also emerged unscathed from the Civil War; the magnificently airy fourteenth century chancel and boss-adorned roof are among the finest examples in the county.

Donkeys grazing on the banks of the Dane at Holmes Chapel.

Set in the southern borders of Cheshire, Audlem is a charming little market town lapped by the infant Weaver, seen at its best from the church perched on a hill overlooking the main street. The fourteenth century chancel and soaring arcaded naves are features of the church, which also has some very handsome furnishings including a pre-Reformation font.

Audlem was the birthplace of Geoffrey Whitney, who brought out a book of "Emblems" in 1586 which he himself described as "A worke adorned with a variety of matter both pleasant and profitable: wherein those that please maye find the fit their fancies: Because herein, by the office of the eie and the eare, the mind may reape double delight throughe holesome preceptes, shadowed with pleasant devices: both fit for the virtuous, to their incoraging: and for the wicked, for their admonishing and amendment".

What, we may ask, is the nature of this book guaranteed to perform all these wondrous things? An emblem was a poem printed in the shape of an object, usually of religious significance, such as a cross, altar or chalice. It is known that Shakespeare had a copy of Whitney's work, which contained 248 emblems.

One needs to spare time to sit by the covered market cross and if possible follow the Weaver up through the area around Cambermere Abbey and Cholmondeley with its bird-rich lakes, remains of a hilltop castle and fine scenery; walk in the Peckforton hills to the source of the Weaver; sit down and spare a thought for the charming little river which has made so many contributions to modern life before entering the Mersey. Blessings have for long been heaped on Cheshire county councils by inquisitive travellers because of their good sense in signing the rivers passing beneath each bridge. The Weaver has many tributaries, but two in particular deserve brief mention, the Dane and the Wheelock.

Close to Congleton on the Buxton road is the stone bridge at Three Shires Head where streams from the cotton grass moors converge to produce the Dane, one tributary arising on the sombre slopes of Axe Edge, littered still by the scars of old mines. The main commodity was coal but some lead was also extracted and smelted on the spot. This area also spawns the Goyt and ravines such as Wildboarclough abound with dippers, ring ouzels and common sandpipers as well as snipe, redshanks and curlews. The boundaries of three pre-1974 counties join here and men from Cheshire, Derbyshire and Staffordshire used to meet on these hills to wager on the outcome of barbarous cock fights. In the old days the constabulary could only operate within the boundaries of their own county, and when cock fighting became illegal the "sportsmen" meeting at Three Shires Head were still sure of at least one escape route. After a flirtation with Bosley reservoir and the deserted village of Havanna, built around a failed cigar works, the Dane flows through Congleton and Middlewich before joining the Weaver at Northwich.

Congleton rare, Congleton rare
Sold the Bible to pay for a bear

What with cock fighting and bear baiting, the Dane seems to have seen more than its fair share of blood sports. It did, however, play its part in industry; a silk mill was established at Congleton as long ago as 1752 and the early prosperity of the town was based on the manufacture of gloves but later concentrated on lace and ribbons. One-time mayor of Congleton was John Bradshaw, the regicide, but a more socially acceptable local was one Sir Thomas Reade who must have been a forceful character because he persuaded the ruler of Tunis to abolish slavery throughout his domains in 1849. Sir Thomas also spent some time on the island of St Helena during the time Napoleon was imprisoned there, the Cheshire man developing the reputation of being able to "handle" the French emperor whenever he became truculent.

A more parochial point of interest to be found in the museum is an unusual leather belt with three bells hanging from it. Known as St Peter's chains, they were used to announced the start of the chimney sweeps' annual holidays in the days when young lads were pushed mercilessly into filthy flues. The connection with St Peter is maintained in the name of the parish church, which is rightly famed for its intricately carved woodwork. The town has two other churches respectively dedicated to St James and to the Holy Trinity, both being erected to serve the expanding population during the nineteenth century.

For those who love wandering around lush countryside studded with working farms, attractive cottages and magnificent old halls, either Congleton or Holmes Chapel would provide a suitable base.

Criss-crossed by a grid of five trunk roads and a grand viaduct over the Dane, Holmes Chapel is a charming spot with touches of the ancient in the form of a fifteenth century church and modern in the sense that it is close to Jodrell Bank Observatory, which in addition to watching the skies also supports a developing arboretum. The observatory with its awe-inspiring planetarium is open to the public.

The temptation to drive straight through Holmes Chapel with its network of roads should be stoutly resisted. Look at the tranquil Dane towered over by the 105 foot high, 60 foot wide twenty-three-arched aqueduct, picnic in one of the spacious parks and examine the church, especially the west tower which still bears the battle scars of the Civil War in the form of pockmarks made by musket balls.

Stone age artefacts, Roman pottery, a mention in the Domesday Book and a medieval church all bear witness to the antiquity of Middlewich, yet another salt town with narrow streets and quaint old buildings. In his eighteenth century travels Dr Johnson described Middlewich as "a mean old town, without any manufactures, but I think, a corporation". This vague and somewhat disparaging description is inaccurate on all counts and "Middlewich-on-Dane" is well worth a protracted visit.

Beyond its suburbs the river is quite substantial, having picked up several other sizeable streams. Some two miles below Middlewich is Croxton, where the River Wheelock merges with the Dane, which then continues to Northwich for its marriage with the Weaver. The Wheelock has its origins on Staffordshire's Mow Cop and runs gently through Wheelock, Warmington and Sandbach, another fine old Cheshire town which is justly proud of its Saxon crosses. It also has suffered its share of brine subsidences and the Sandbach flashes are regular haunts of birdwatchers in search of the rare birds which seem to find them irrisistible.

It is now time to leave the River of Salt and to return to the Mersey itself.

CHAPTER NINE

The Cheshire Bank

A LEISURELY journey around Stanlaw, Ellesmere Port, Eastham, Port Sunlight, Birkenhead and Bidston, Wallasey and New Brighton will show that where thick woodlands clothed the hillsides less than a century ago, the modern world has arrived in just one short word—oil! Other industries are present, of course, but it is the tangle of terminals, the persistence of pipes and the odour of oil which typify the Wirral bank of the Mersey today.

We may have to look hard for forgotten history and beauty here, but they who seek shall surely find.

> Stanlaw! where I hope to lie
> When my hour shall come to die,
> Hard thy lot and brief thy fame
> Still thou teachest by thy name –
> Stan and Law together blending
> Name all neighbour names transcending.
> Law is hill—I lift mine eyes
> To the hills beyond the skies
> Stan is stone—O! Corner stone!
> What art thou but Christ alone.

This lovely verse was almost certainly written by a homesick monk faced with the prospect of having to leave his abbey, built on land given to the Cistercians by John de Lacy in 1178. Neither de Lacy, who perished on a Crusade, nor the abbey built on Stanlaw Point thrived. The abbey ground was subject to flooding at the point where the River Gowy, the last of the major tributaries on this bank, joined the Mersey. After particularly disastrous floods and gale damage in 1279 and a fire two years later the monks moved to Whalley, much more pleasantly situated on another patch of de Lacy land in the fertile Ribble Valley. Despite one monk's lament, the move must have been welcomed by the majority, for Stanlaw Point must have been a tough spot to scrape a living. Part of the monastery's income came from the right to collect "wrecum maris", the washed up seaweed being burned to produce alkali before the Leblanc industry evolved.

The Gowy rises in the Peckforton hills and begins its journey to the Mersey by flowing through Beeston with its lovely black and white cottages snuggled below a towering 500 foot rock topped by the gaunt ruin of a castle built in 1220. Despite being wrecked in the aftermath of the Civil War, its crumbling walls, moat and well, 366 feet deep, remain as monuments to its former glory.

Beyond Beeston the Gowy was crossed by the Roman Watling Street, heading from Chester to Manchester, and another imperial route from Chester, this time to Wilderspool, forded the river at Bridge Trafford. The Gowy, which forms the southern boundary of old Wirral, and the Mersey once mingled beneath the very walls of the ill-fated Stanlaw Abbey, but during the construction of the ship canal the Gowy had to be culverted underneath the canal.

A few stones still remain of the abbey, but Stanlaw Island is now a huge oil terminal where many work but few live. Huge umbilical-like pipes drain oil from tankers and carry it ashore for processing; smoking is banned because safety is paramount. The first oil dock was not begun until the middle of the First World War and the real development has taken place only since the early 1950s. Fumes and pipes are not popular with people, people are not popular with birds, and so Stanlaw is a

The River Gowy at Stanlaw.

surprisingly rich haven for wildlife. Some unsightly oil does spill occasionally, but not so often as you might think, and waders such as knot and dunlin twist and turn in flight, their pale underparts catching the sunlight and flashing like a signal beacon.

Prior to the canal age there was no Ellesmere Port, only a fragmented population centred on the hamlet of Whitby keeping body and soul together by farming and fishing. In 1793 an Act of Parliament granted the shareholders of what became the Shropshire Union Canal permission to slice a cut "from the River Severn at Shrewsbury in the county of Salop to the River Mersey at or near Netherpool in the County of Cheshire". Work proceeded at a hectic pace and the first stage, called the Ellesmere Canal, opened to traffic in 1795. Thus the industries thriving in the town of Ellesmere deep in Cheshire acquired their own port, and an exit to the sea.

Few places have been so maligned as Ellesmere Port. In 1847 William Mortimer insulted it by writing that "There is probably no town in the Kingdom, possessed of equal advantages, which presents so dull—so gloomy an appearance". More than a hundred years later Norman Ellison chipped in that "it is probably the busiest and most prosperous place in Wirral: it is also crude and ugly. The growth of industry has been too rapid; there has been no time for civic planning or vision". Growth was indeed rapid, producing a town of 60,000 people from a population of fewer than 200 within 150 years, and this was due not to one canal but two. The Manchester Ship Canal brought much trade and a steam ferry connection to Liverpool, but eventually Ellesmere Port, like others on the Mersey, declined. Crude and ugly towns are not frightened of work, and oil refineries and a large Vauxhall car plant have both created jobs.

The present town planners are more considerate towards the environment and Ellesmere Port is showing signs of maturing with age. It is pleasing to see that with the establishment in 1976 of the Boat Museum among the old structures of the Shropshire Union Canal, some buildings designed by Telford are being preserved. Brightly coloured barges and canal boats bob in bays protected by restored lock gates. The sound of saw, hammer, chisel and plane echoes through the repair sheds as tugs, wide boats, ice breakers with specially strengthened bows, narrowboats, day boats and butty boats wait their turn to be restored and painted. There is a restaurant and a shop and the old stables of the canal horses once more look spick and span. In the summer horse-drawn barges operate a passenger service along the canal.

From the museum there are magnificent views over the old basin where sailing ships waited to be unloaded into the canal boats. Beyond is

the Manchester Ship Canal and the Mersey. Downstream is the historic but now industrialised area of Eastham where the ship canal locks into the Mersey.

The village of Eastham is about a mile away from the shore and the old ferry. Even though Eastham is only about a hundred feet above sea level there are spectacular views over the Mersey towards Otterspool, the dockside buildings of Pier Head and the two cathedrals, the shape of the catholic building accounting for its affectionate name of "Paddy's Wigwam". Those of us with a nostalgia for the sea get a lump in the throat as ships from distant ports nose their way slowly towards the ship canal locks.

There is more greenery around Eastham than along the rest of the Wirral bank, which has been largely built up during the last fifty years. Fortunately Eastham woods are safe from development, having been bought by the local council in 1934. Hordes of Liverpudlians had been flocking over on the ferry for a good day out here since the middle of the nineteenth century. The ferry closed down in 1929, but the old iron pier remains and provides a superb viewing platform. There was a ferry here as long ago as 1509; steps down to Job's Ferry can be seen cut into the rock leading down to the beach just north of the iron pier, from where the monks based at Birkenhead Priory ferried folk across the Mersey.

In the summer of 1984 I descended the steps and picked my way among oily globules on the muddy beach, expecting to find nothing.

138

Opposite: The Boat Museum at Ellesmere Port, at the terminus of the Shropshire Union Canal. The modern container depot can be seen in the background.

Right: Ellesmere Port in the days when the docks were full of sailing ships, Mersey flats and canal boats transferring their cargoes.

From among the stones and piles of washed-up seaweed I disturbed five turnstones, which flew low over the waves of the river, and a ringed plover trotted away along the pebbles, earning its local name of stone-runner. I turned a few stones myself and was delighted to find the depressions teeming with life. Shore crabs, shrimps, sand hoppers and tellins all turned up, and among the seaweed was a fine collection of shells including mussels, cockles, top shells and a lovely example of pelicans foot, with its shell shaped like a bird's foot with its webs spread.

Returning to the iron pier, I wandered beyond the old ticket office built in 1857 and across the road to the imposing thee-storeyed Ferry Hotel, built in 1846 to cater for travellers waiting for a storm to abate. The journey across to Liverpool before the days of steam could take more than four hours and must have been quite dangerous, even when steam did replace the oar. One interesting story, which I suspect is true, concerns the building of a second bar quite separate from and now across the road from the main Ferry Hotel. It is said that the masters stayed in the main hotel and the servants kept to their own alehouse, thus retaining the class barriers even when storm-bound.

What the "upper classes" would have thought of the goings-on in Eastham Woods goodness only knows. Here was a zoo, complete with bear pit and monkey house, plus old fountains and a dazzling display of azealeas and rhododendrons which once delighted thousands of visitors. There was even a theatre in the area, which was known as the Richmond of the Mersey. Unfortunately a minority—it is always a minority—behaved badly and the place fell out of favour, destroyed by its largely undeserved reputation. The area is now a delightful country park with a most unusual visitors' centre in the form of an old forge removed from Flaybrick, near Bidston. A trail leaflet guides walkers through a carpet of maytime bluebells spangled with the nodding white heads of wood anemone and stitchwort. Colourful fungi are equally delightful in the autumn.

Tree creepers spiral their way up the trunks of magnificent oaks, and jays feed on the acorns. Bank voles and long-tailed field mice will be seen by those who visit the woods early or stay late and are prepared to spread a few unsalted peanuts or oatmeal in a quiet spot. The trees are magnificent, especially in autumn, their beauty enhanced by views of the river through the branches as the leaves fall. Eastham has one tree famous above all others, a gaunt and ancient yew found in St Mary's churchyard, reached through its lovely lych-gate. Its precise age has not been calculated but a safe range would seem to be between 1,000 and 1,500 years old. It could well have been part of the ancient forest which once covered the Wirral, this one tree having survived because it, or perhaps its immediate ancestor, was a place of pagan worship. This sacred place was taken over by the Christians who first worshipped under the tree and then built their own church beside it.

Port Sunlight must be the cleanest town in the world since it is named after a soap which brought a fortune to its inventor, who used his wealth

Attractive houses and public gardens in W. H. Lever's Port Sunlight.

much more wisely than most. William Hesketh Lever was born in Bolton in 1851 and took a house in Warrington in 1885 before devoting his life to making a new kind of soap which people would buy. He stopped using tallow and substituted vegetable oil, improving both texture and smell. He improved the latter even more by adding lemon-scented citronella oil, designed an attractive packet and launched "Sunlight" soap. With demand outstripping supply and his Warrington works soon proving inadequate, he found a new site at Lower Bebington with a handy stream and an outlet via Bromborough Pool to the Mersey and the world. At Bromborough Pool Price's Patent Candle Company already had a "model village" which had housed their workers since 1853.

William Lever was not a man to do things by half. His scheme for his workforce in 1888 is a magnificent tribute to a man who could have treated his people as shabbily as many of his contemporaries, but chose not to do so. Port Sunlight was designed with great care, the works and the houses being dovetailed perfectly together. No two streets were alike; around each and every corner there lurks a new and delightful surprise provided by the design of the houses (almost 1,400 of them), plus more than fifty buildings devoted to leisure activities.

Nobody could have worked as hard as William did without full support from his wife, and when Lady Lever died in 1914 William planned the Lady Lever Art Gallery in her memory; it was opened in 1922. Again this was no ordinary effort; rather was it just what you would expect from a man whose last Christmas card, sent in 1924, less than six months before his death in May, 1925, had printed upon it:

Give me always a goal to try for,
Let me toil till my days be spent,
Give me a dream to fight and die for
And I shall be content.

What dreams there are within this building with as much floor space as Westminster Abbey. It is well worth a visit to see the magnificent collection of Wedgwood pottery and the paintings by Gainsborough, Reynolds, Constable and George Romney, who was born at Dalton-in-Furness and worked a great deal in Kendal. Stipulating that the gallery was to be freely open every day except Christmas Eve and Good Friday, William lovingly produced a place to linger in and to return to time and time again. The business which he founded still thrives today as part of the giant Unilever empire, and many employees still live in Port Sunlight and enjoy its fine library, neat pub and, of course, one of the country's finest art galleries right on their doorstep. A visitors' centre and bookshop have recently been established.

It is something of a contrast to drive out of Port Sunlight towards

New Ferry and Birkenhead, now such an integral part of the industrial complex lining the bank of the Mersey, with very few places left for the walker to get near the waterside.

Beyond Port Sunlight lies Rock Ferry, now spoiled by a new road slicing straight through it. Here at No 26 Rock Park lived the American Consul Nathaniel Hawthorne, who in 1853 described the village he grew to love, despite his earlier reservations regarding the dull wet climate.

> This is the most beautiful day of the English winter—clear and bright with the ground a little frozen and the green grass brightly growing along the waysides at Rock Ferry, and sprouting up through the frozen pools. England is for ever green.

The pier at Rock Ferry played host to many a famous ship, including the *Indefatigable*, an iron ship used to train sailors, and another even more famous vessel, the *Conway*, a wooden frigate which was presented to the City of Liverpool by the government in 1859. She broke her back while under tow on her way for a refit in 1953. To this vessel came John Masefield to begin his sailing apprenticeship in 1890 when he was only thirteen. I wonder if he thought of the dear old Mersey when he later came to write *Sea Fever*:

> I must down to the seas again, to the lonely sea and the sky,
> And all I ask is a tall ship and a star to steer her by
> And the wheel's kick and the wind's song and the white sail's shaking.
> And a grey mist on the sea's face and the grey dawn breaking.

Hawthorne's house still stands in Rock Park as one of a series of gentlemen's houses built across the water away from the pressures of Liverpool business. The park still leads down to the Old Rock and beyond it the New Ferry with its Great Eastern Hotel, which still retains some of its Victorian elegance.

Close by is a fascinating spot called the Magazine, reached along a narrow lane with a disused railway running alongside it. No wonder it is a lonely spot, because it was here that ships were provided with their gunpowder, it being far too risky to load explosives in the confines of a crowded harbour. This must have been very handy at the time that Laird's yard was building fighting ships.

Ellesmere Port, Port Sunlight and Birkenhead are often classified together as towns built from scratch during the industrial boom of the nineteenth century. This description does not quite fit Birkenhead, because as long ago as 1150 a Benedictine priory was built in the eastern corner of the summit of Birchen Head. Were there birch trees here and did they give the settlement its name? Or was it because the Priory was close to the head of the small river Birken which trickles down into the Mersey from here? We shall never know, but at least the large town has

Liverpool with its Anglican and Roman Catholic cathedrals seen across the Mersey from Rock Ferry, with a coastal tanker making its way upriver to load.

retained its small priory. The Corporation took over the ruin in 1896 and in recent years have restored it sufficiently for it to be used for services following the demolition of the nearby St Mary's Church. The twelfth century chapter house is in a fine state of repair and there are impressive remnants of the crypt, the great hall and the kitchen.

The monks had a genius for selecting vantage points, and their Birchen Head land, given by Hamo Mescy, third Baron of Dunham Massey near Altrincham, overlooked the Mersey to the east and the pools of Tranmere and Wallasey to the south and north respectively. It was essential that the Monks had a good view of the river since one of their main functions was to provide a ferry service to the Lancashire side, landing near a little spot called Liverpool. Edward II granted the first official charter in 1318 and Edward III issued a second in 1330, the toll charges being recorded at this time. It was best to travel on market day without luggage when the fare was a farthing. Any other day you paid a

143

ha'penny, unless you were carrying a pack when the fee doubled to a penny. A mounted man also paid a penny unless the beast was burdened, when tuppence was the price. The crossing was a tough one, but the prices were far from cheap in those days and the monastery must have become very rich.

Initially the monks reserved the toll for one journey and the Lord of the Manor of Liverpool was allowed to charge for the return. Even after the dissolution of the monasteries there were two recipients but in the eighteenth century a careless mistake on the Liverpool side allowed their lease to lapse; whichever way you cross the river today you pay the boatman on the Birkenhead side.

Near the priory is the portal of the Mersey tunnel, from which cars emerge into daylight after a journey of nearly three miles under the river. Opened by King George V in 1934, Queensway was built by Liverpool City Council. I expect the loss of ferry income provided some of the incentive to build the toll tunnel, which cost £7,450,000, only £2,500,000 being provided from central funds. Kingsway, the second road tunnel, opens at Wallasey and will be described later. The authorities must have blessed the Birkenhead tunnel during the Second World War when so much pressure was placed on shipbuilding and other industries on both sides of the river.

The only underground railway in England and Wales other than the London "Tube" is the Liverpool to Birkenhead line, which opened in 1885, five years before the first "tube"—yet another first for Birkenhead, which has many claims to primacy. The first Scout troop was initiated here after Baden-Powell gave a lecture in January, 1908, on his Boer War experiences. Birkenhead was, in 1860, the first European city to install a tramway system invented by a man called Train. Between 1842 and 1847 Sir Joseph Paxton, the landscape gardener and architect, transformed an evil-smelling swamp into the world's first public park whose 225 acres, a riot of colour in summer, still provide welcome relief in a riverside town with no access to its river. Birkenhead's park was carefully studied by Frederick L. Olmsted when he designed New York's Central Park, sections of which clearly show an English influence.

Birkenhead is renowned for shipbuilding in general and Cammell Laird's yard in particular. The fortunes of shipbuilding have been at a very low ebb in recent years, but sea-based employment has been maintained at Tranmere's oil terminal, which can handle the largest tankers. The history of shipbuilding on the Birkenhead side of the Mersey is just as interesting to American historians as to those in this country. William Laird set up the company in 1824 and within five years the yard had built one of the first iron vessels and also the steel paddle boat which years later carried Dr Livingstone up the Zambesi. Cammell Laird's fame as warship builders actually began by costing the British Government £3 million in compensation and prevented Laird, by then Mayor of Birkenhead, from getting the knighthood for which he had been strongly tipped, all because Liverpool backed the wrong side in the American Civil War. It is hardly surprising that Liverpool chose to throw in its lot with the southern states since the city's prosperity had been founded on the slave trade on the outward run and the trade in cotton and rum on the homeward trip. Whether out of conscience or merely to spite Liverpool, Manchester backed the Union. When hostilities started in 1860 James Dunwody Bulloch, the Confederate agent, was welcomed in Birkenhead, whence the steamship *Alabama* with its skilful American Captain Raphael Semmes and a crew made up of local sailors set off for America. As a commerce raider she is said to have accounted for more than fifty Union vessels during 1862 and 1863. After having been at sea almost two years the *Alabama* was sunk off the coast of France in June, 1864, by the U.S.S. *Kearsage*. Another fascinating link between Birkenhead and the American Civil War is that the Confederate flag hauled

Liverpool's Anglican cathedral seen across the roofs of Cammell Laird's shipyard at Birkenhead.

down from the mast of C.S.S. *Shenandoah* in the Mersey for a refit, on 10th November, 1865, was the last to be struck; so the hostilities ended not in America but in the Mersey.

After the war came the recriminations; the British Government paid the United States government £3 million compensation and the Mayor of Birkenhead remained Mr William Laird and never got his knighthood.

Rising two hundred feet above the industrial sprawl of Birkenhead towers the council-owned Bidston Hill, a pine-covered eminence ablaze in summer with large expanses of fragrant gorse. From the summit, enclosed as a deer park as long ago as 1407, there are magnificent views over both the Dee and beyond the Mersey towards the Ribble. The tiny River Fender can just be seen before it is swallowed up by Wallasey Pool. Ancient civilisations were certainly aware of the strategic value of this hill and there are rock carvings, said to be those of a sun and moon goddess, which some experts think may be two thousand years old.

Apart from the profusion of wild life and a seemingly ever-present breeze, the summit supports three fascinating structures. Firstly there are a series of supports which once held flagpoles, secondly there is Bidston observatory, and thirdly a most intelligently sited windmill. In these days of advanced telecommunications the flagpoles are no longer of use, but in Youngs' *Perambulations of the Hundred of the Wirral*, published in 1909, it is written:

> Formerly there were fifty eight flagpoles arranged along the summit which were used for signalling the arrival of merchant vessels in the offing, and telescopes were directed to the summit from the old churchyard in Liverpool for information.

Bidston Observatory was built in 1866 to help set ships' chronometers as accurately as possible before they began a long voyage, success depending on first-rate navigation. Initially this had been done in Waterloo Dock, Liverpool, but increasing levels of atmospheric pollution made dependable observations of sun and stars impossible. Was it coincidence, I wonder, that placed the new observatory so close to the carvings of the goddess of Sun and Moon? From 1873 a lighthouse built to replace a 1771 model has stood near the observatory but the light has not burned since 1908.

Nowadays the observatory has the imposing title of The Institute of Oceanic Sciences. Its reputation for excellence was based initially on a calculator which could work out tidal movements anywhere in the world after a gestation period of whirring, whizzing and clanking. It was still delighting visitors to Liverpool Museum long after it had been replaced by a computer, but in 1984 it was returned to the observatory.

I was once strolling high on the slopes of Bidston Hill when I overheard a family loudly discussing the stupidity of having a windmill designed to grind corn on the top of a hill. Below us the sun was beating down and not a breath of air was stirring, but on the hill a cool breeze would have flown any kite and turned any mill sail. Although it has not needed to produce flour since 1875, the attractive white tower mill is visible for miles around and is a popular focus for picnickers.

The village itself, much quieter since the by-pass road was built in the 1970s, has some attractive and historic buildings, not least interesting being Bidston Hall, one of the homes of the Earls of Derby, who ruled the Isle of Man. Built of grey sandstone in 1620 (it replaced an earlier Tudor house of 1535), it was confiscated by Cromwell because of the

An old view of Bidston Mill, out of use for more than a hundred years.

support given by William, the 6th Earl, to his King. In 1649 Parliament offered a free pardon in exchange for his support. Writing from the Isle of Man, Derby penned a thunderously courageous reply:

> Sir,
> I received your letter with indignation and scorn. I scorn your proffers, disdain your favour, and abhor your treason, and am so far from delivering up this Island to your advantage that I will keep it to the utmost of my power to your destruction. Take this for your final answer and forebear any further solicitations, for if you trouble me with any more messages, I will burn the paper and hang the bearer.

In the event it was Derby who was executed, after he had sailed for England to join the army of Charles II on its way from Scotland; he was captured at the Battle of Worcester in 1651, taken to Bolton and had his head hacked from his shoulders.

Now privately owned, Bidston Hall is just one of the many attractive buildings clustered around the hill which give a clear feeling of what life must have been like on the Wirral coast when folk looked to the Isle of Man in the west. Masefield put it rather well, although his context was rather different:

It's a warm wind, the west wind, full of birds' cries;
I never hear the west wind but tears are in my eyes.

More than a hundred thousand people still live in the complex of Wallasey, which has absorbed Leasow, Moreton, Poulton, Liscard, Seacombe, Egremont, once another area where gunpowder was loaded into ships, and the much-maligned seaside resort of New Brighton. Once the home of red deer and wild ox which roamed the forest and also of the beaver which a thousand years ago gnawed through trees on the Mersey banks, Wallasey now has few trees but a magnificently airy promenade all the way to New Brighton with splendid views over to Liverpool, surely the loveliest waterfront in the world.

The derivation of the name Wallasey seems rather strange until you look at a map. Waelas-eig means "strangers' island", and if viewed from the sea the inlet of the Mersey which forms Wallasey Pool makes it look as if it is an island. Prior to the 1790s Wallasey had its own racecourse but this has long since gone, the area now being an impressive series of gardens providing fresh vegetables for the Liverpool markets.

The Ferry across the Mersey made so famous by the Beatles, Jerry and the Pacemakers and other groups which dominated the world pop scene in the 1960s still pulls into the Seacombe landing stage as it has done at least since the seventeenth century and possibly long before. Before steam, the journey by rowing boat must have taken hours, now in the days of diesel it takes a mere fifteen minutes or less. In its heyday this ferry carried thirty-two million passengers in a year, now with competition from two road tunnels and a rail link the numbers are much smaller. Economics rule the waves these days, not Britannia or Sentiment, and the ferry cannot consider itself safe from closure unless it is utilised. How about a sail and a day trip to New Brighton? Stand on Seacombe pier and look down the Mersey towards Birkenhead. There are only oil terminals, so turn around and follow the straight promenade to New Brighton, with magnificent views to sea and the smell of brine and ozone in your nostrils. Once a healthy seaside resort with a tower to rival Blackpool, New Brighton became very sick a few years ago and nearly died, but the patient is now showing some signs of recovery.

New Brighton in 1830 was one huge sandhill, with nothing but lovely views. This would be quite enough for most of us, but James Atherton had other ideas when on retirement from his business in Liverpool he bought 170 acres, intending to establish a watering place to attract a few

An old photograph of
New Brighton tower,
built in the closing
years of the nineteenth
century.
Ann Murphy

rich people. What happened in fact was that the enterprise attracted huge numbers of poorer folk, who travelled across on the steam ferries. The profits were the same, but the effect on the "new" Brighton built at Wallasey was almost ruinous. Sideshows cheated everyone and prostitution, thieving and brawling became commonplace. In 1889 a critic named Sulley was able to write that

> Along the shore is a narrow unsafe promenade, called Aquarium Parade, but perhaps better known as 'Ham and Egg Terrace', the favourite resort of the Liverpool and Lancashire trippers and roughs .... With more visitors and few trippers New Brighton would be more flourishing.

It was true to say that New Brighton was more vulgar than Blackpool at this period and that what it needed was a thoroughly respectable

149

gimmick. In 1897 the idea came—a 621 foot tower, 103 feet higher than Blackpool's and thus Britain's highest structure. The Tower opened amid great celebration in 1900. It is difficult to understand why the £120,000 project failed to work, but it was never a success. During the 1914-18 war the structure was neglected, and most of the upper part was demolished in 1921, but the theatre and ballroom continued to function until destroyed by a fire in 1961.

When the container docks were built at Seaforth changes in currents affected New Brighton's ferry dock, which has now gone, and sections of its magnificent beach became unsafe for swimming. The safe areas are now marked with yellow and red flags, while lifeguards patrol the beach. For those who are still wary, an outdoor swimming pool which can accommodate four thousand swimmers does a fine trade in summer.

Projecting into the Mersey estuary from the mass of amusement arcades and hotels is Perch Rock, which has a most unusual history. The first navigational aid in the Mersey was the Beacon perch, and foreign ships passing it had to pay a toll of sixpence. Perch rock, an outcrop of red sandstone, could be reached at low water but took a fiercesome battering during the frequent storms. What was needed was either a substantial lighthouse or a fort. In 1825 both were provided, but the light is no longer needed and the fort never fired a shot in anger. The cannon fired practice rounds during the nineteenth century, and if legend is to be believed local fishermen earned a casual income by returning the cannon balls which they recovered from the Mersey sandbanks. The fort now houses a cafe and caters for an increasing number of visitors who arrive via the new road tunnel opening at Wallasey.

The view from Perch rock around into the Dee estuary or inland to the sandstone cliffs riddled with caves, some still entered by trapdoors in the gardens of houses and once used by smugglers, is fascinating. New Brighton, like the rest of the Wirral, has much to offer the holidaymaker and is beginning, after almost a hundred and sixty years, to come to terms with itself.

CHAPTER TEN

The Liverpool Shoreline

THE SMELL of the seaside ozone becomes progressively stronger until we reach Pier Head, which is often battered by high tides driven into the Mersey from the Irish Sea.

A vulgar city of riots, always in conflict with authority and crouched alongside a filthy river: that is the description often given of Liverpool. This is the second-hand opinion of those who have never been, who also glibly state that things are getting worse. Those of us who love this city with its magnificent buildings know different. The river is cleansed daily by the sea, which has a tidal range greater than anywhere else in the country with the sole exception of Southampton. The folk will "pull your leg" but are as friendly as you deserve. The water is no dirtier than that in most other big ports, and a great deal cleaner than some I could mention both in Britain and throughout the world. A bracing wind keeps the air fresh and the salt spray is invigorating.

The last lap of the Mersey's journey to the sea takes us from Widnes through Hale, Speke, Otterspool, the great and historic dockland complexes of Liverpool itself, and away to Formby Point. Beyond Formby lies Southport and another of Lancashire's river arteries, the Ribble, which has been much less important than the Mersey. The same is true of the Dee estuary across the Bay and beyond the Wirral; once the Dee silted up and virtually cut off the port of Chester during the seventeenth century the success of Mersey's port was assured.

As we leave Widnes only one stream of any size trickles into the Mersey, the ten-mile-long Ditton Brook which drains Childwall, Gateacre, Huyton, Roby, Halshead and Halewood, all ancient villages now swallowed by suburbia. One village which has survived virtually intact is Hale, overlooking Dungeon Banks on the river. Hale is famous with ornithologists because of its duck decoy and mud flats, while it is the delight of historians who can see old cottages and think of an ancient hall. Here, too, seekers after the bizarre will thrill to the true story of the Child of Hale. But here above all is beauty and agriculture within a stone's throw of a huge city. Hale is in the midst of one of Lancashire's prime wheatgrowing areas, while thousands of daffodils are grown here and via the new motorways soon find themselves in florists' shops throughout England. The village and the surrounding countryside have long been

151

famous for market and flower gardens run by small-scale operators. Palmer, writing in 1946, obviously loved Hale:

> In every soul there is a natural love of brightness and beauty, therefore modern Christmas has its message of flowers. The shops are radiant with crysanthemums, roses and anemones of all colours, in all purity, in strength of bloom. Romance there is behind this display of glorious flowers and foliage—the romance of an industry which the gardeners contend was established in the Garden of Eden. The industry has many branches around Hale, where hundreds of acres are under glass .... Men and women are employed all the year round on the flower industry. As Christmas approaches, the four months season of the chrysanthemum matures. Then comes the time of the hyacinth, daffodil and tulip.

It is not only the gardener who has cause to bless the area around Hale, for ornithologists gather around Hale Point and its disused lighthouse, the most southerly point in Lancashire, to watch magnificent flying displays by dunlin, knot, oyster catchers and redshanks. In the autumn of 1979 a great deal of controversy was generated when heavy pollution just west of Hale Point killed large numbers of birds, including over a thousand dunlin. The British Trust for Ornithology in its report on this subject agreed that heavy metals, lead in particular, were responsible. The experts' conclusion was that the lead had probably been lying in the silt of the Mersey for many years and had been disturbed by

The lighthouse at Hale Point.

dredgers operating on the river. This lead had then been taken in by invertebrate animals such as lugworms and ragworms, which in turn were eaten by the birds.

An event such as this should certainly worry us, but we must surely take heart from the increasing numbers of birds now present on the Mersey and from the fact that pollutants entering the river these days are under more careful control than ever before. Cormorants still catch flatfish off Hale Point, shrimpers still fish off the Mersey Bar and wading birds are increasing in numbers.

Equidistant between the ruins of Hale Hall and Ditton Brook is the now restored duck decoy, which at one time guaranteed a ready supply of fresh meat for local tables. The hall kept its own decoy book from 1800 onwards, recording more than a thousand birds taken in some seasons and as many as one thousand five hundred in a good year. According to Whittaker's *British Duck Decoys* during the period from 1900 to 1917 no fewer than 6,545 teal, 800 mallard and 221 wigeon were caught. The decoy is pentagonal in shape and surrounded by a moat crossed by swingbridge. The pond is sheltered by a belt of trees, and each of the five curving channels opening off the pond funnel into cages which get gradually narrower. Skilful little dogs followed their masters' whistled instructions and either lured or manoeuvred the wildfowl to their doom. Decoys must have been a vital part of the rural economy before the advent of accurate guns. The actual date of construction of the Hale decoy is the subject of some argument among historians, some saying 1613, others 1631.

Although Hale is not specifically mentioned in Domesday it can be recognised from a description given of four manors within the parish of Childwall. It is thought that the origin of the name is from the Old English Halh, meaning a nook, and therefore a good geographical description.

To describe Hale Hall accurately needs care since three buildings exist which have in some form or another and at some time or another functioned as the manor house. In 1203 Richard De Walton was given land at Hale by King John, and when he died without issue his sister, who had married a member of the Ireland family, inherited . From the Court Leet records, which fortunately have survived, we know that many buildings in Hale were thatched and that a fire officer could be appointed by the Constable to watch over them.

There is a 1465 record regarding the Ford Toll which reads "John Jackson of the North country, Edward of Little Legh, in the Parish of Preston, and with him, Nicholas Grayson, and one, said to be of Northope, in Wales passed over Hale ford with horses cattle and sheep and was arrested by Henry Penultune baylive, of the said village for their stallage, for toll". Another entry which throws some light on the unpolluted state of the Mersey in former years refers to the Lord of the Manor at Hale having the right to a tithe of fish. Instead of a percentage, the two sides agreed that all fish caught on a Friday belonged to Hale Manor. The entry for 4th August, 1728, in the reign of George II reads "There was caught att Hale on fryday the abovementioned day of ye month, being the Tyth day, 30,000 herrings and upwards".

The Ireland family was directly associated with Hale until 1675, and it was they who built the first hall, a baronial mansion on an impressive scale, and surrounded it with a deep moat. The precise date is not known when "The Old Hutte", as it became known, was built, but we do know that it was somewhere between 1617 and 1626, and that it was considerably altered in 1674. The last true-blooded Ireland died childless in 1675, but the Ireland-Blackburns were still in residence until they sold out in the 1930's. The Fleetwood-Heskeths bought Hale Hall in 1947, but by then the poor old house was too far gone to save, so the family took over the Parsonage overlooking the village green and it is this seventeenth century building of delicate pink sandstone which is now called the Manor House.

Sir John Betjeman wrote one of his typically witty poems about The Manor House Hale. Two verses in particular seem to catch the essence of the place:

In early twilight I can hear
A faintly ticking clock
While near and far and far and near
Is Liverpool baroque.

The Manor House, the Green, the Church
From Runcorn to West Kirkby
You will not find howe'er you search
So sweet a rus in urbe

Old Hale has a mainly modern church, through no fault of its own. There has been a church on this site since the eleventh century, but in the fourteenth a new building with a splendid sandstone tower was erected. The tower survived both the extensive reconstruction of 1758 and a terribly destructive fire in 1977. When the church reopened in May, 1980, the roof had been lowered, giving the tower an even greater dignity than it had before. The chaplains of the parish can be traced back to 1270, and the records show that Hale had its share of characters. None was more fascinating than one of humble birth who astounded the Royalty of the day. This was John Middleton, affectionately known as The Childe of Hale.

On the gravestone is written "Here lyeth the bodye of John Middleton, the Chylde of Hale. Born A.D. 1578 Dyed A.D. 1623". Anything but a child, Middleton was at the age of forty-five a giant measuring nine feet three inches in height; his hand was seventeen inches long and the breadth of his palm eight-and-a-half inches. Some doubt about his size was expressed during the eighteenth century, and after much argument the body was exhumed, being kept for some time at Hale Hall before decency prevailed and Middleton's remains were returned.

John Middleton had the strength to match his size, and Sir Gilbert Ireland decided to take him to the court of James I, no doubt more with the intention of drawing attention to himself than of advancing the giant John, whose origins were humble. Middleton was well clothed for the trip "with large ruffs about his neck and hands, a striped doublet of crimson and white; round his waist a blue girdle embroidered with gold; large white plush breeches powdered with blue flowers; green stockings; broad shoes of a light colour, having red heels, and tied with large bows of red ribbon; just below his knees bandages of the same colour with large bows; by his side a sword suspended by a broad belt over his shoulder, and embroidered as his girdle with blue and gold, with the addition of a gold fringe upon this edge".

At Court the Childe, put in the ring against the King's wrestler, devastated the poor fellow in quick time, dislocating his thumb to boot. Many courtiers were not amused at seeing their favourite beaten by a bumpkin from the country, and James sent the Childe home with £20 in his pocket as a parting gesture. On the return journey to Hale the party halted at Brazenose College, Oxford, which was dominated by Lancastrian scholars, and during his stay the college had painted a life-size portrait of the Childe, which still hangs in the library. Another life-size portrait may be seen at Speke Hall.

Surrounded by industry and a substantial housing estate, and separated from the Mersey by the runway of Speke airport, stands Speke Hall, one of the finest Tudor houses in Britain. There is a record in the Domesday Book of a dwelling on the site belonging to Uctred the Saxon, but the Norris (Le Noreis) family was in control by the thirteenth century. The present building is reached by a bridge over what was once a wide moat and under a magnificent stone porch bearing the inscription "This worke 25 yards long, was wolly built by Edw. N. Esq., Anna 1598". The spacious courtyard in the centre is dominated by two magnificent yew trees, affectionately known as "Adam and Eve".

The banqueting hall is rich in intricate carved panelling said to have been brought from Holyrood House in Edinburgh. Another Scots connection is an attractive tapestry brought back from Scotland as booty following the Battle of Flodden Field. In the parlour is a stucco ceiling which has been dated around 1605, the technique having been introduced from Italy during the reign of Henry VIII. Despite working in a notoriously difficult material, the craftsmen—English, apparently—produced surprisingly life-like representations of flowers and fruit.

Wherever you go in this magnificent building, now owned by the National Trust but leased to Merseyside County Council, the feeling of gracious living follows you, especially, in my opinion, in the great hall, where the Norris family would entertain their guests. One little device reminds us that the sixteenth and seventeenth centuries were often troubled and dangerous. Guests left alone in the great hall would no doubt talk together, and a series of narrow and well-concealed openings lead to the eaves, where a trusted servant could listen and report back. Here is the origin of our word "Eavesdrop". The hall also has its share of priest holes and a number of observation points and bolt holes, evidence that the family were staunch catholics.

In 1731 the Norris family ran out of male heirs and Mary Norris married Lord Sidney Beauclerk, the fifth son of the Duke of St Albans. The family paid little attention to Speke and it fell into a serious state of decay, a situation not helped by local farmers who were allowed to use the house. Speke Hall was saved by the Watt family who made a fortune out of the shipping business, based mainly on the slave trade. Once more the family at Speke ran out of lusty males and when Miss Adelaide Watt died in 1921 she left the house in trust to the Norris family, which she had taken the trouble to trace. In 1943, however, the house passed to the National Trust; it can now be said to be in safe hands.

From the hall signed walks lead through Stockton's Wood, full of magnificent old trees separated by banks of colourful rhododendrons originally planted to give cover for game. The trees hide the modern factories which surround Speke, bird song fills the woodlands, pheasants call from the bushes and rabbits hop along the open rides. A sweeping lawn leads to a high bank, at the top of which a footpath runs alongside the main runway of Speke Airport, which was built in 1933 but has been expanded greatly in recent years. Before the airport was built the grounds of the hall led down through water meadows carpeted with flowers to the Mersey. A glance downstream from the top of today's high bank reveals Liverpool's industrial skyline but with a surprising number

Liverpool's International Garden Festival in August, 1984, with Cammell Laird's shipyard at Birkenhead visible on the far side of the river.

of bright spots, including Otterspool, the garden festival site and the maritime museum.

Otterspool Park and promenade, complete with bowling greens, masses of flowers and a breezy walk alongside the river, is a perfect example of what a city can do with its rubbish if it sets its mind to it. What the locals thought about the area during its construction is thankfully not recorded. In the early 1930's a footpath, usually covered with mud, seaweed and increasing quantities of oil, followed the river bank at Otterspool, no doubt once a feeding area for what is now one of Britain's rarest mammals. Then came the plans for the first Mersey Tunnel. What was to be done with the rock?

In 1932 the council grasped the nettle, built retaining walls alongside the river and inside them dumped both rock and the increasing amounts of domestic refuse, thus solving two problems at once. Although the war interrupted the scheme the first stretch was opened to the public in 1950 and the promenade is now over two miles long. Much of this book has been written in the open air, and I am writing these words sitting on a bench overlooking the sparkling, clean Otterspool promenade, watching the river lapping against the supports and pausing occasionally to share my lunch with a black-headed gull.

Between Otterspool and Pier Head, Liverpool, lies another area which was once a derelict site used as a tip, but from 2nd May to 14th October, 1984, was home to the International Garden Festival. It was hoped that when the festival was over some of the site would remain and be connected to Otterspool.

The Liverpool International Garden Festival was the largest event to take place in Britain since the Festival of Britain in 1951. Many people have criticised the festival as a waste of money which will have no lasting effect, but such critics have missed the point. The 250 acres chosen for the gardens was one of the most unattractive areas in the city, and a real blot on the Riverside area of the Mersey. In six weeks the reclamation team removed 600,000 tons of silt from the disused Herculaneum Dock and poured in a million and a half tons of sand to produce a space to park as many as ten thousand cars. An out-of-date oil terminal complete with underground tank and two large jetties was demolished and a total of 800,000 tons of rubble removed and used to build artificial hills. All this was accomplished between October, 1981, and March, 1982, when the task of planting 250,000 trees began. By November, 1982, work had started on sewage and water systems, plus a sea wall.

This ambitious project was finished in February, 1983, but by then the decaying material buried beneath was producing methane; it has been estimated that some two-and-a-half million therms of gas will be produced each year, and plans are afoot to make use of it after the festival has ended. Whatever happens to the site, some of the attractive areas overlooking the river, including Priory Wood, will remain. The esplanade will eventually form part of the link from Otterspool to Pier Head. The Festival Hall will provide Liverpool with a much-needed sports and leisure centre, while some of the remaining land will be used for industrial and domestic buildings. Long after the flowers have faded and the media have lost interest Liverpudlians will remember the festival with affection. Here is part of Liverpool's future sandwiched between two slices of her past, Speke Hall and the utterly compelling maritime museum.

Situated close to Pier Head, the Merseyside Maritime Museum first opened its doors in July, 1980. Although it is not expected to be complete until 1989, it is already in September, 1984, an exciting exhibition of the life of the port, with indoor and outdoor displays which can only be really appreciated after several protracted visits. The ocean gallery including the builders' scale model of the ill-fated *Titanic* is an imaginative piece of planning. It is the restoration of the docks and of some splendid old ships

The Albert Dock, Liverpool, which became derelict with changing trends in shipping and has now become the subject of a conservation project.

such as those that once turned Masefield's thoughts to the sea which is the real joy:

> A wind's in the heart of me, a fire's in my heels,
> I am tired of brick and stone and rumbling waggon wheels
> I hunger for the sea's edge, the limits of the land,
> Where the wild old Atlantic is shouting at the sand

The Albert Dock section opened to the public in August, 1984, just in time for the Tall Ships Race which brought back so many memories of earlier days of sail in Liverpool when cotton and, dare I say it, the slave trade were kings. It has to be admitted that Liverpool's early prosperity was based fair and square on this unwholesome trade:

> Get slaves honestly if you can,
> And if you cannot get them honestly
> Get them.

Sail training ships in the old dock at Liverpool at the time of the Tall Ships' race in August, 1984.

This old saying was inscribed on the jacket of a book called *Liverpool and Slavery*, published in 1884 but written at an earlier date by "Dicky Sam", who wished to remain anonymous for fear of retribution. He wrote

> The system of trade carried on by the Liverpool African trades ran as follows:— Ships were built and fitted to carry slaves; the cargoes consisted of Manchester and Yorkshire woollen goods, hatchets, cutlasses, gunpowder and trinkets, pistols, muskets etc from Birmingham and Sheffield; these they bartered for slaves—men, women and children—on the west coast of Africa; they then carried their cargoes of slaves to the West Indies, who were sold for specie, sugar, and rum and the latter commodities were sold in Liverpool, thus making three profits to the merchants in one voyage.

The one bright spot is that "Dicky Sam" was not alone in his dislike of this most unsavoury but profitable enterprise, and Liverpool eventually played its part in the abolition of the slave trade. It took courage for some to bite the hand that fed them. It is to be hoped that the maritime museum eventually devotes a gallery to slaving; it would do us all good to see for ourselves how the frightened Africans were packed together for their nightmare trip, which so many failed to survive.

Liverpool did not become a city until 1880 and did not receive or deserve any mention in the Domesday Book. In the eleventh century it would have been nothing more than a collection of fishermen's hovels governed from West Derby. It was King John who in 1207 signed the Letters Patent raising Liverpool to the status of a borough and a potentially influential port. Why did John do this when he was not renowned for doing anything for anyone other than himself? The answer is that the greedy monarch had his eye on Ireland and needed a convenient port other than the one he already had at Milford Haven, which was becoming a problem because the Welsh did not like him much and neither did the Earl of Chester, whose attitude effectively closed another port. There were so few people living in Liverpool at that time that it did not matter much whether they liked the king or not. Here then was the beginning of Liverpool's love-hate relationship with Ireland, which has been evident ever since. What the old seal given by King John looked like we do not know, because it was lost during the siege of Liverpool in 1644, but there seems little doubt that St John's Eagle would have been shown prominently, almost certainly carrying a twig. By the time the expanding town got around to replacing its coat-of-arms in 1797 they remembered the old bird carrying something in its beak but they forgot King John—who liked him, anyway? The artist therefore drew a rough sketch of a local bird, a cormorant, and gave it a piece of laver (seaweed) to carry. Here then is the now world famous Liver bird, which even the official guide book of the city looks upon with friendly humour:

> This most famous, tufted, long necked, long legged, web footed emblem of the city may lack a proven pedigree but is nothing if not regal to look at and the generally accepted theory is that whilst it never came out of any egg it can boast royal origins.

Liver birds now stand supreme overlooking Pier Head, which has been the focal point of the city's prosperity since the heyday of sail. Before the days of tunnels many ferries crossed to the Wirral, dodging between commercial ships and huge luxury liners on their way to and from America. From here the poor left to seek their fortunes; those who had made them returned first class to see their homeland. No account of riverside Liverpool, however superficial, would be satisfactory without some reference to the ferries, three tunnels and three lovely buildings overlooking Pier Head.

Ferries across the Mersey have been part of riverside life at least since 1130, when the Benedictines operated the crossing from the Lancashire shore to Birkenhead. Ferry rights were jealously protected and by the eighteenth century the Runcorn, Woodside, Tranmere, Monks and Eastham routes were all doing good trade, as in later years were Rock Ferry, New Ferry, Egremont and eventually New Brighton. Steam ferries came early; the *Liverpool Mercury* announced in 1815 that

> On Wednesday last, about noon, the public curiosity was considerably excited by the arrival of the first steamboat ever seen on our river. She came from the Clyde, and in her passage called at Ramsey in the Isle of Man, which place she left early in the morning. We believe she is intended to ply between this port and Runcorn, or even occasionally as far as Warrington. The cabin will contain about 100 passengers.

Why go to Runcorn? Runcorn was at that time a thriving bathing resort. At first this steam vessel was an unreliable if amusing novelty, but gradually the increasing reliability as well as the increasing size of the steamers made the ferry journeys safe, and more comfortable, and the bigger steam ferries were commodious enough to carry large vehicles. In 1889 the Reverend Richard Postance wrote a booklet called *Old Liverpool* in which he discussed the development of ferries.

> A hundred years ago "crossing the water" was a serious and risky undertaking; the ferry boats for the accommodation of passengers were small and inconvenient, and the ferry houses were quite in keeping with them. There were ferries at Woodside, Lower Tranmere, Seacombe, Rock Ferry, New Ferry and Eastham, and the most usual place for landing on the Liverpool side was the George's pier. Passengers were conveyed in small boats of five or six tons burden, with accommodation for about fifteen people, and it is easy to imagine that in boisterous weather, and with a strong tide running, the voyage was at times a perilous one. The first steam ferry-boat to cross the Mersey was a strange looking craft called the *Etna*, which commenced to run in 1817. It was a kind of double boat, with one paddle-wheel in the middle. Although this vessel was a great advance upon the old

Queensway, the
original Mersey
tunnel opened in
1935.

sailing ferry boats, the dangers of embarking and landing passengers were not
diminished, as at low tide the steamer could not come alongside the steps, and small
boats had to be used. This dangerous and inconvenient landing was a source of
frequent complaints, and at length a "gut" was made, into which the steamers ran
and landed their passengers on a slip, which was only a little less disagreeable than
the steps, and accidents, more or less serious, were of frequent occurrence. The next
move was the construction of a small stage running in and out of a tunnel according
to the state of the tide. This landing-stage difficulty was at length solved by the
building of the George's floating stage in 1847 by the Dock Board at a cost of
£60,000; it was 500 feet long and 80 feet wide.

The rapid increase of traffic, and the necessity of further accommodation for all kinds of passenger steamers led to the construction of the Prince's Landing-stage by the Dock Board, at a cost of £120,000; it was 1,002 feet long and 80 feet wide. The stages were connected with the quays of the river wall by means of hinged girder bridges, so as to rise and fall with the tide. The two landing-stages were united in 1873-4, and formed a magnificent promenade deck, 2,060 feet in length; the total cost of the whole structure, with the improved bridges and approaches, being £373,000. Shortly after its completion, it was, to everyone's amazement, destroyed by fire, July 28, men were at work, and owing to the highly inflammable nature of the timber which had been saturated with creosote, the efforts of the firemen were absolutely useless: the fire could not be reached, and nearly every portion of the stage was ruined, the loss being about £250,000. The work of reconstruction was soon proceeded with, and the landing-stage was in a very short time, once more ready for its enormous traffic.

Now that the Mersey tunnels carry road and rail traffic only two ferries are left running from Liverpool, the Seacombe Ferry landing at Wallasey and the other at Birkenhead. Even these are now threatened with closure but it is to be hoped that for once sentiment will prevail and an eight-hundred-year-old tradition of a ferry across the Mersey will be continued. As the river becomes more of an amenity the ferries could easily fulfil the secondary function of adding to the flotilla of pleasure craft which are a pleasant addition to Merseyside life. The ferries must not be allowed to disappear into oblivion as was the case with the Liverpool Overhead Railway, which operated from 1893 to 1956. The Birkenhead Tunnel was so successful that the ferry traffic declined alarmingly after the opening of Queensway in 1935, and in 1971 a second tunnel, Kingsway, was built from Liverpool to Wallasey. These tunnels now offer a quick way into the city, as too does the railway system. But the most exciting views of the city of the Mersey are still only possible from the prow of the ferry, or from some other ship in the river.

The pierhead trio—the Mersey Docks, Cunard and Liver buildings—have been recently cleaned so that they reflect sunlight into the large square which still combines business with pleasure. Here is a bus station, harbour, rose garden, picnic area and general meeting place for "scousers".

Arnold Thornley designed the offices of the Mersey Docks and Harbour Board, which opened their doors in 1907, in the style of a Renaissance palace, complete with a cathedral-like dome. The interior reinforces this impression. An octagonal hall soars towards the dome and four layers of arched galleries wind around it.

The Royal Liver Building, facing ships arriving from the United States, home of the skyscraper, was Aubrey Thomas's reply on behalf of the old country. Built between 1908 and 1910, it was the first multi-storey building to use reinforced concrete. Two huge clock towers topped with domes on which perch Liver Birds are visible from miles out to sea and have symbolised home to four generations of mariners.

The last of the magnificent three to be built was the Cunard office, designed in the Italian style but with fascinating Greek overtones; it was the combined effort of Willink, Thicknesse and Davis and was completed during the First World War. Also visible from the river are two cathedrals, one Anglican, the other Catholic.

The Anglican Cathedral took from 1904 to 1978 to complete, is twice as large as St Paul's, has a tower 466 feet above sea level and is the largest Anglican church in the world. Only the cathedrals of Seville, Milan and St Peter's in Rome are larger than this, almost certainly the last Gothic-style cathedral which will ever be built. The Catholic building, officially called The Metropolitan Cathedral of Christ the King, is often affectionately called "Paddy's Wigwam" because of its tent-like shape. This unusual but compelling building was completed in 1967. Frederick Gibberd, who designed the "Wigwam", was a Nonconformist while Giles Gilbert Scott,

The yacht *Lively Lady* and rum casks in the Merseyside Maritime Museum at Liverpool. In the background can be seen the buildings on the Pier Head.

who was responsible for the Anglican building, was a catholic—it could surely only have happened in Liverpool!

The site of the present-day pier head is somewhat altered from the heyday of Liverpool's old docks, the seaward view being partially blocked by the recent developments needed to convert Liverpool into a container port. Seaforth Docks were modernised during the 1970's and can handle bulk carriers of 75,000 tonnes. A walk around Bootle Docks, which retain many eighteenth and nineteenth century warehouses, or into the old town, reading the street names, will soon bring the nostalgia pouring back. Cotton Street, Jamaica Street, Oil Street and Canning Street reflect places, trades and people. Liverpool requires a book to itself.

The last point of land in old Lancashire is Formby Point but the Mersey officially ends, swallowed by the sea, at Liverpool Bar, thirteen miles from St George's landing stage at Pier Head. This channel is

Looking out over the River Mersey from the Pier Head at Liverpool. It was here that passengers used to embark for America.

marked by buoys, but great care is needed since the sands are notoriously mobile. For many years huge blocks of stone were dropped into trenches to build underwater retaining walls in an effort to prevent yet further disasters on a coast already littered with wrecks.

Before joining the sea, however, the Mersey has one more tributary to swallow, the small but interesting River Alt. The Alt has two main sources, one in Croxteth, the other in Knowlsley Park. Both these stately homes are now major tourist attractions, with fairgrounds and fun and with Knowlsley Safari Park bringing the roar of the African jungle to mingle with the song of an English blackbird. A far cry indeed from the traditional meander of the Alt, easing itself gently through fertile fields and watermeadows around Sefton, close to the hare coursing route of the Waterloo Cup and the Grand National Course at Aintree.

The Alt Valley was dominated for centuries by the Molyneux family, who in 1747 became the Earls of Sefton. Sefton's sixteenth century church was built on the site of a religious house in use before the Norman Conquest. The church is renowned for its magnificent woodwork, especially the intricately carved screen and monuments to the Knights Templars. The church spire is a landmark for miles around—and also a seamark.

The Alt reaches the Mersey at a point equidistant between Crosby and Formby. Crosby was originally a tiny village, now appropriately called Little Crosby and remaining aloof from development. The name derives from the Norse "the place of the crosses", and one of these crosses still remains. Although development has reached Crosby, its history is still there to be seen. The prosperous Liverpool merchants, wishing to live away from the clamour of the docks but still wishing to watch their ships arriving from foreign parts, built beautiful Georgian houses at Crosby. These have wrought-iron balconies overlooking the Crosby channel. The area known as Waterloo developed during the 1820s and today offers bowling and putting greens, a heated indoor swimming pool, an outdoor children's paddling pool plus a model boating lake.

I chose to write the last lines of this book on board a small boat heading out from Crosby. There behind a ridge of flower-rich dunes lies Formby, and close to the Alt estuary is Hightown, its surrounding dunes used occasionally as a firing range. A look back at Liverpool is essential, for the city and its river are for ever linked. It is a lovely thought that a few years ago the Bishop of Liverpool took a huge iron ring into the estuary and dropped it overboard, symbolising the marriage of a river and a city. After a long courtship, the two have lived together happily for many years, and still show no signs of discontent.

Bibliography

P. Anderson. *Tame Valley Wildlife*, Greater Manchester Council, 1981.
G. Atkinson. *The Canal Duke's Collieries*, Neil Richardson, 1981.
W.E.A. Axxon. *Annals of Manchester*, John Heywood, 1887.
W.E.A. Axxon. *Lancashire Gleanings*, Tubbs Brook and Chrystal, 1883.

O. Bott and R. Williams. *Man's Imprint on Cheshire*, Cheshire County Council, 1975.
C.T.G. Boucher. *James Brindley, Engineer 1716-1772*, Goose and Son, 1968.
P. Bowes and M. Patry. *Eccles, a Collection of Old Photographs*, City of Salford Cultural Services.
C. Bracegirdle. *The Dark River—The Irwell*, Sherratt, 1973.
K. Burnley. *Portrait of Wirral*, Robert Hale, 1981.

G.A. Carter. *Warrington and the Mid Mersey Valley*, Marten, 1971.
J. Champnew. *Lancashire's Early Industrial Heritage*, Lancashire County Planning Dept., 1983.
J. Corbett. *The River Irwell*, Abel Heywood, 1907.
J. Corbridge. *A Pictorial History of the Mersey and Irwell Navigation*, Morton, 1979.
A. Clayre (Ed). *Nature and Industrialization*, Oxford University Press, 1982.
A. Crossland. *Looking back at Urmston including Flixton and Davyhulme*, Willow, 1983.

G.E. and A.R. Davies. *The River Irwell and its Tributaries*, John Heywood, 1890.
"Dicky Sam". *Liverpool and Slavery*, Bowker and Sons, 1884.

Norman F. Ellison. *The Wirral Peninsula*, Robert Hale, 1955.

B. Falk. *The Bridgewater Millions*, Hutchinson, 1942.
L. Faucher. *Manchester in 1884*, Abel Heywood, 1884
Ron Freethy. *Man and Beast, the Natural and unnatural history of British Mammals*, Blandford, 1983.
H. Forrester. *Twopence to Cross the Mersey*, Bodley Head, 1974.
P. Fox. *Old Saddleworth*, Peter Fox, 1982.

Hilda Gamlin. *Twixt Mersey and Dee*, Liverpool, 1897.
D.D. Gladwin. *The Canals of Britain*, Batsford, 1973.
Grayling. *The Bridgewater Heritage*, Bridgewater Estates P.L.C., 1983.
W. Greenwood. *The County Book—Lancashire*, Robert Hale, 1951.

Charles Hadfield. *British Canals: An Illustrated History*, David & Charles, 1969.
C. Hadfield. *Macclesfield Memoirs*, Hadfield, 1984.
J. Hanmer. *Western Peakland*, Willow, 1980.
J. Hanmer, A. Lee, W. Marsden. *Walking Around Marple*, Hanmer, 1983.
A. Hayman. *Mersey and Irwell Navigation to Manchester Ship Canal 1720-1887*, Bridgewater Cruising Club, 1981.
Frank Hird. *Lancashire Stories* (Two volumes), T.C. and E.C. Jack, 1911.
P. Howell Williams. *Liverpolitana*, Merseyside Civic Society, 1971.

T.S. Lightfoot. *The Weaver Watermen*, Cheshire Libraries and Museums, 1983.
Liverpool Heritage Bureau. *Buildings of Liverpool*, Liverpool Planning Dept., 1978.
D. Lyddon and D. Marshall. *Paper in Bolton: A Papermaker's Tale*, Sherratt, 1975.

C. Makepeace. *The Manchester Ship Canal*, Hendon, 1983.
John Masefield. *Collected Poems*, Heinemann, 1923.
H. McKnight. *The Shell Book of Inland Waterways*, David and Charles, 1975.
J. McInniss. *Birkenhead Priory*, Countrywise Ltd, 1983.
C. Moore. *Old Maps of Cheshire*, Moore Maps, 1981.

D.E. Owen. *Cheshire Waterways*, Dalesman, 1979.

W.T. Palmer. *The River Mersey*, Robert Hale, 1944.

W. Robinson. *The Mersey and the Irwell*, B. Taylor & Co, 1888.

J.N. Slater. *A Brewer's Tale*, Greenall Whitley, 1980.
Alan Smith. *Salford as it was*, Hendon, 1983.
H.F. Starkey. *Schooner Port. Two Centuries of Upper Mersey Sail*, Hesketh, 1983.

G.H. Thomas. *The Minutes Tell the Story: Lymm 1895-1974*, Lymm Local History Society, 1980.
V.I. Tomlinson. *Salford in Pictures*, Morten, 1974.

University of Liverpool. *The Changing Face of Liverpool 1207-1727*, Liverpool Archaeological Society, 1981.

K. Warrender. *Exploring Longendale*, Willow, 1980.
Cyril Wheaton (unpublished). *A Brief History of Glazebrook*.
K. Williams. *Ghost Ships of the Mersey*, Countrywise Ltd., 1980.
P. Williams and J. Hayes. *Warrington as it was*, Warrington Museum, 1982.
Wilmslow Historical Society. *Three Sundays in Wilmslow*, Wilmslow Historical Society, 1981.

Ince power station and the marshes on the Cheshire side of the Mersey in the late evening of a July day.

Index

Illustrations in bold type.

A

Adlington, 89
Aintree, 167
Albert Dock, **159,** 160
Alice in Wonderland, see Daresbury
Alt, river, 167
Anderton lift, 116, 128-130, **128, 129**
Arden Hall, *see* Castle Hill
Ashton-on-Mersey, 29
Ashton-under-Lyne, **9,** 12, 33, **65**
   Canal, 62-63, **65**
Audlem, 130, 132
Axe Edge, 133

B

Bacup, 38-42, **40, 41, 42**
   Naturalists, 39
Bank Hall, 105
Barton, 34
   aqueduct, **60,** 66, **66**
Beeston, 135
   Castle, 90
Bennet, Abraham, 72
Bewsey Hall, legend of, 98-102
Bidston, 135, 147-148
   Hill, 146
   Observatory, 146
   Windmill, **147**
Birch Hall, see *Waltzing Weasel*
Birch vale, 10
Birkenhead, 135, 142, 144, 146, 162
   Priory, 138, 143, 144
Boat House Inn, 34
Boat Museum, Ellesmere Port, 137, **138**
Bobbin, Tim, 36, 54, **54**
Bog asphodel, 2
Boleyn, Anne, 84
Bollin, river, 42, 71-88, **73,** 89
Bollin Point, 37, 65, 70, 88
Bollington corn mill, 88
Bosley reservoir, 133
Bottoms reservoir, 4, 72
Bowden, 86-87
Brabyns Park, 11
Bradshaw Brook, 48
Bradshaw, John, 23, 113

Bramhall Hall, 24-26, **24**
Bridgewater Canal, 33, 59-61, **62,** 88,
   104, 111
Brindley, James, 59, 72
Brine extraction, 120, 122
Britannia Coconut dancers, **39,** 40
Bromborough Pool, 141
Burnley, 41, 42
Butterfly, cabbage white caterpillar, **125**
Butterfly, small tortoiseshell, **123**
Byle, river, 52

C

Cadishead, 92, **92**
Cambermere Abbey, 133
Carr brook, 12
Carrington, 37
Carrs, The, 84-85
Castle Hill, 18
Cat and Fiddle Inn, 6, 8, 71
Caves, Mersey Gorge, **25**
Chadkirk Country Park, 11
Chapel-en-le-Frith, 8
Cheadle, 29, 30, 89
Cheeryble brothers, *see* Grant Brothers
Chelford, 89
Chester, 2, 70, 98, 111, 135
Chew brook, 12, 15
Childe of Hale, 155
Childwall, 151
Chinley, 8
Cholmondeley, 130, 133
Chorlton, 29
   brook, 33
   Water Park, **31,** 31, 32
Collier, John, *see* Bobbin, Tim
Combs Moss, 10
Combs reservoir, 10
Compstall Navigation, 69, 70
   mill, 4, 70
Congleton, 23, 133
Cornbrook, 65
Crawshawbooth, 42
Croal, river, 38
Croal Valley Project, 47ff, 64
Cromwell's Bank, 109

Crosby, 167
Crowden Brook, 3
Croxteth, 167
Cunard Building, 164, **165**
Curlew, 1, **74**

D
Dane, river, 127ff
Daresbury, 60
Davyhulme, 34
Dean, river, 71, 89ff, 133
Deansgate, 52
Dee, river, 70, 150
Deerplay Moor, 38
Delamere Forest, 124
Delph, 14
Denshaw, 14
Derbyshire Bridge, 6, 8
Dickens, Charles, 43
Didsbury, 29
Dipper, 5
Diggle, 13
Diggle brook, 13
Ditton brook, 151
Dobcross, 13
Domesday Book, 4, 76, 79, 117, 127, 153, 155, 161
Duck decoy, Hale, 153
Dukinfield, 12, **17**
Dunham Massey Hall, 88

E
Eastham, 135, 138
   Country Park, 139
   Ferry, 139
   Locks, 66, 68
Ellesmere Port, 70, 135, 137, **139**
Errwood Hall, 8
Errwood reservoir, 7
Etherow Country Park, 4, 5, 70
Etherow, river, 1-5, **3**
Eustace Carey 'flat boat', **130**
Evans, Bramwell, 84

F
Fiddlers Ferry, 70, 107-109, **107**
Flixton, 29, 34, 48
   House, 34-35
Formby, 167
Frodsham, 116, **117,** 124, 125
   Marshes, 119, 125

G
Gallows yard, 11
Garden Festival, Liverpool, **157,** 158
Gateacre, 151
Gilbert, John, 59
Glazebrook, 90, 94
Goodshaw Chapel, 42
Goose, Canada, 4
Gowy, river, 135, 136,**136**
Goyt bridge, 6, 7
   river, 5-12, 42
   valley, 6, **6**
Goytsclough Quarry, 7
Grant Brothers, 43-44
Greenfield, 17
Greg, Samuel, 85, 86

H
Hale, 151-154
   lighthouse, **152**
Halton Castle, 109
   Court-Leet, 110
   library, 110
Handford, 89
Harecastle tunnel, 70
Havanna, 133
Hayfield, 9
Hightown, 167
Hollins Green, 59, 90, 94
Holmes Chapel, **127, 132,** 134
Huddersfield Canal, **18,** 63
Huyton, 151
Hyde, 12
   Anne, 19
   Edward, 19
   Hall, 19

I
Ince power station, **169**
Irk, river, 38, 48, 51-52, **55,** 56, 68
Irlam, 90-92
   Ferry, 37
   steelworks, 37, 90
   weir, **37,** 90
Irwell, river, 38-58, **92**
Irwell-Mersey Navigation, 48ff, 64
Island Church, **124**

J
Jackson's Boat, 32-33, **32**
Jenkin Chapel, 7

Job's Ferry, 138
Jodrell Bank Observatory, 114

K

Kin, river, 9, 11
Kinder Scout, 9
Kingfisher, 4
Kingsley, Charles, 1
Kingsway, *see* Mersey Tunnel
Kirkwood, 11
Knowlsey Hall, 167
  Safari Park, 167
Knutsford, 89

L

Laddow Rocks, 3
Latchford, 98
  Canal, 111
Leeds and Liverpool Canal, 64
Legh family, 74, 76-77, 80
Leigh, 64, 94
Limey water, 42
Littleborough, 52
Liver bird, 161-162
Liver Building, 164
Liverpool, 64, 70, **143, 145,** 156ff
  Anglican cathedral, 138
  Catholic cathedral, 138
Lymm, 60

M

Macclesfield, 7, 75-78, **77, 78,** 80, 85
  Canal, 64, 72
  Forest, 11, 71
Mallard, 4
Manchester, 4, 21, 64
  Ship Canal, 29, 34, 37, **58,** 64ff, 71, 94,
  119, 137
Maritime Museum, Merseyside, 159-160,
  165
Marple, 4, 11
Marple aqueduct, **10,**11
Marthall brook, 89
Medlock, river, 13, 38, 48, 56-57, **57,** 65,
  68,
Mersey Docks and Harbour Board Build-
  ing, 164
Mersey ferries, 137, 138, 139, 143, 148,
  162-164

Tunnel, 144, **163,** 164
  Valley Project, 26ff
  View, 123, 124
  Way, 12
Middlewich, 70, 89, 117, 133
Milnrow, 36, 52, 54, **54**
Mobberley brook, 89
Moses Gate Country Park, 47
Moss, Fletcher, 31
Mossley, 12, **18,** 28ff
Mottram St Andrew, 82-83
Mount Manisty, 68
Mow Cop, 134

N

Nantwich, 130-132
New Brighton, 135, 148-150, 162
  tower, **149**
New Ferry, 142, 162
Northwich, 116, 122, 127ff, 133
  salt museum, 127, 128
Norton Priory, 61

O

Ogden, river, 43
Oldham, 60
Old Moseley Hall, 30
Orchid, Marsh, **95**
Otter, **46,** 47
Otterspool, 138, 158
Overhead railway, 164

P

Partington, 92
Peak Forest Canal, 11, 64
Peckforton Hills, 135
Pedley brook, 89
Peel, Robert, 42
Perch Rock, 150
Pickford, Thomas, 7
Pier Head, Liverpool, 138, 151, 159, 162,
  166
Pomona docks and gardens, 68, 69
Port Sunlight, 135, 140, **140**
Pott Shrigley, 89
Prestbury, 78-82, **80, 81, 83**
Prestolee aqueduct, 48, **49**
Prestonbrook tunnel, 70

Q
Quarry Bank Mill, *see* Styal mill
Queensway, *see* Mersey Tunnel

R
Radcliffe, 42-46, 53
Rainow, 89
Ramsbottom, 43
Rawtenstall, 41, 43
Reddish Vale Trail, 19
Red Hole, 2
Rhodeswood reservoir, 4
Ribble, 36, 135
Ridgegate reservoir, 72
Ringway Airport, 86
Rixton, 95
Roaches trail, 19
Rochdale, 37, 52, 54
    Canal, 60-62, **63, 68**
Roch, river, 38, 52, 54, 94
    pollution of, **45, 56**
Rock Ferry, 142, **143,** 162
Rock Hall, 47
Roman lakes, 11
Runcorn, 60, 61, 111, **113,** 162
    and Latchford Canal, 66
    ferry, 106, 115
    gap, 105, 106, 111, 115
    shipbuilding at, **108**
    transporter bridge, 111, 112
Runcorn-Widnes bridge, **112**

S
Saddleworth, 12, 13
St Helens, 106-107, 120
St John's Church, *see* Jenkin chapel
St Mary the Virgin, Stockport, **22,** 23
Sale, 29
    Hall, 33
    Water park, **26,** 33, **33**
Salford, 48
    Junction Canal, 68
Salterbrook, 2
Salt industry, 119ff, **121**
Sankey Navigation, 70, 94, 106, 107, 111
Sefton, 167
Sett, river, 9
    valley trail, 10

Shelf Brook, 3
Shining Tor, 8, 89
Shropshire Union Canal, 70, 137
Sparrow pit, 8
Speke airport, 155
Speke Hall, 155-156
Sphagnum moss, 2, 6
Spike Island, 113, **114**
Spodden Water, 53
Stalybridge, 12, 20
Stanlaw, 135, **136**
    Abbey, 135, 136
Stockport, 1, 8, 12, 20-25, **22,** 25
Stretford, 60
Stubbins, 43
Styal, 71, 86
    mill, **85,** 86
Sudley Walter, 53
Sugar Well, 19, 20
Sutton aqueduct, 72
    Hall, 72
Swallow, 5
Swans, **94**
Swift, 5
Swinshaw Hall, 42

T
Tame, river, 12-20, 94
    valley improvement scheme, 14
Tall ships, **160**
Taxal, 10
Teal, **96**
Tegg's Nose Country Park, 74
    reservoir, 72
Thelwall, 90, 94, 97
Three Shires Head, 133
Toad Lane, Rochdale, 55
Todd brook, 8, 11
Tong, river, 48
Torside reservoir, 4
Trafford Park, 34
Tranmere, 162
Trentabank reservoir, 72
Trent and Mersey Canal, 69, 119
Twinney Bridge, 89

U
Uppermill, 13
Urmston, 29, **29,** 34, 36

INDEX

V
Valehouse reservoir, 4
Vernon Park Museum, Stockport, 24

W
Wallasey, 135, 148
Waltzing Weasel, 10
Warburton, 90, 92-94
Warmington, 134
Warrington, 37, 70, 88, 90, 98
  Academy, **103**
  bridge, 98, **103**
Water Babies, The, 1
Waterloo, 167
Weaverham, 126-127
Weaver Navigation, 116, 119
Weston Church, 124, **124**
  Point, 119, 126
Whaley Bridge, 8, 10
Wheelock, river, 134

White, Nancy, 89
Whittaker Park Museum and Art Gallery, 41
Whittington, Dick, 7
Widnes, 70, 112-115, 151
Wildboarclough, 42, 113
Wilderspool, 98, 117, 135
William the Norman, 4
Wilmslow, 71, 84
Winsford, 119, 130, 131
Woodcock, 8
Woodhead reservoir, 4
  tunnel, 2
Woodside ferry, 162
Woolston, 96, **97**
  weir, 106
  Eyes, **97**
Worsley, 59-60
Wrigley, Ammon, 12, 43